Sorcery and Gold

A Story of the Viking Age

Rosalind Kerven

Illustrated with wood engravings
by Simon Brett

CAMBRIDGE
UNIVERSITY PRESS

Cambridge Reading

General Editors
Richard Brown and Kate Ruttle

Consultant Editor
Jean Glasberg

PUBLISHED BY THE PRESS SYNDICATE OF THE UNIVERSITY OF CAMBRIDGE
The Pitt Building, Trumpington Street, Cambridge CB2 1RP, United Kingdom

CAMBRIDGE UNIVERSITY PRESS
The Edinburgh Building, Cambridge CB2 2RU, United Kingdom www.cup.cam.ac.uk
40 West 20th Street, New York, NY 10011-4211, USA www.cup.org
10 Stamford Road, Oakleigh, Melbourne 3166, Australia
Ruiz de Alarcón 13, 28014 Madrid, Spain

First published 1998
Reprinted 1999

Printed in the United Kingdom at the University Press, Cambridge

Typeset in Concorde

A catalogue record for this book is available from the British Library

ISBN 0 521 46878 7 paperback

Contents

"Let the man who opens a door
be on the lookout
for an enemy behind it."

– *from* HÁVAMÁL,
a poem of the Viking Age

CHAPTER 1

Strangers from the Night

It should have been spring; but it wasn't.

Snow flurried on the hilltops, it crusted in the valleys. Around our farm the ground was so hard that an axe could scarcely dent it. Every track, every path lay unused and lonely, treacherous with drifts, potholes and ice.

One frozen evening after supper, the great wooden door of our house shook with such a frenzied knocking that we all jumped from our seats in surprise.

"A visitor!" exclaimed Uncle Egil. By instinct, his hand reached out for a sword.

We all held our breath and waited. Before long, the knocking echoed again through the long hall, and a muffled voice called: "Is anyone at home? Is there a bowl of soup to spare, and a corner to sleep in for a poor, weary traveller?"

Uncle Egil strode uneasily across to the door. The firelight caught the taut muscles of the fist that gripped his sword; his other hand was lost in shadows as he fumbled with the heavy iron bolt.

"Who is it?" he cried. "How many of you are there? Have you any honest business to be out on a night like this?"

For a few moments, no reply came. Then: "I am alone," called the voice, so faintly that we had to strain to catch it. "My business is to . . . to do no harm to anyone. My name is Ruadh, good sir, and I'm a poor and honest man."

Uncle Egil turned to us.

"Well, shall I –"

"Oh, come along," scolded Aunt Thorhalla, "he's a foreigner, Egil: you can tell by his name and his stuttering way with words. What quarrel could we have with him? For pity's sake, let the poor man in to the warm!"

So Uncle Egil released the bolt and swung open the huge, creaking door. A man stepped over the threshold, bringing with him a shock of icy air. The door shut behind him with a thud.

The stranger was short and wiry, and well past youth. His long, tatty beard was more streaked with grey than black; as he came into the light, tiny icicles dripped from the corners of his moustache. He was wrapped from head to foot in a vast, hooded cloak of shaggy sheepskin that had been torn and patched so often you could scarcely tell its shape.

He stood there, shivering and rubbing his chapped hands together, looking round at us. I stared right back at him, and noticed at once an odd light in his eyes, a curious summer softness.

"Thank you, sir," he said to Uncle Egil. "God will bless you."

"Let's shake the ice out of your cloak and sit you by the fire," said Aunt Thorhalla, bustling him over to the hearth. "Just look at you, you're turning blue with cold. Whatever made you set out on the road in foul weather like this?"

He squatted down and held his hands to the flames while my aunt gave orders to the servants: "Hurry up, let's have some soup and a few slices of mutton!" They all hurried off good-naturedly – except for Kjartan, the boy slave, who hung back, scowling at Aunt Thorhalla's back before deigning to follow suit.

"Mistress," said Ruadh, the colour coming into his cheeks, "you're as kind as an angel!"

Uncle Egil sat down in his high-seat in the centre of the room, still fingering his sword nervously.

"Where are you from, foreigner?" he asked.

"I come from the south," said Ruadh, "from Ireland." His voice was as soft as his eyes, tripping lightly over the words with his curious accent, as rain patters over fallen leaves.

"What do you want with us here?" said Uncle Egil, stiff as a fire-iron.

"I'm looking," said Ruadh, "for my son." He leaned confidingly towards my uncle. "You understand me, friend? You know what a son is to a man? You know how the heart sings to hear his step? Then you'll understand how I wept on the day that my only son was stolen from me."

Aunt Thorhalla coughed. "We haven't got a son," she said drily.

"But you have a daughter," said Ruadh, looking at me.

"Ingrid's our foster daughter," said Uncle Egil. "We took her in to honour my brother – her father – when he died a hero's death. She's a good girl, and a joy to us, it's true."

I longed to hear Ruadh's story; but now he looked up eagerly at the sound of the servants returning.

The footsteps did not bring his dinner after all. Instead, the slave boy Kjartan came running across the hall, his wild black eyes gleaming bright.

"Master, Mistress!" he cried hoarsely. "There's a great band of men on horseback riding towards the farm!"

"What?!" Uncle Egil, who had only just begun to relax, started up again, rigid in every limb.

"Say that again, boy, and don't you dare to lie!" cried Aunt Thorhalla, seizing him by the shoulder.

"Mistress, on my life, I was fetching things from the outside store when I heard voices and horses in the distance. They're riding fast! Coming closer!" His thick, dark mane of hair was plastered to his forehead; the words came out in short, breathless gasps.

"Were they armed?"

"I think I heard metal clinking. I couldn't see much. The moonlight isn't strong."

"What a night!" exclaimed Aunt Thorhalla.

My uncle paced the floor, pulling wretchedly at his beard. "This is outrageous! What could possibly bring such . . ."

His eye fell upon Ruadh, who still sat there, massaging the blue ends of his fingers and staring calmly into the fire.

"Are they after *you*, foreigner?"

"My friend?"

"What have you done? Are they chasing you out?"

Kjartan was back, hissing, "Master, Mistress, they're only a few minutes away!"

"Well, if they're after him – and what else could it be? – the man must hide," declared Aunt Thorhalla. "We're tangled with him now, and so be it." She took a key from the bunch that jangled at her side, and threw it to me. "Ingrid, take Ruadh at once to the earth-house, and make sure you shut the door fast. Then hurry back here to wait with us."

There was no time for fear: I grabbed a lamp and beckoned to Ruadh to follow.

We had scarcely left the main hall before it began to echo again with knocking. The sound was terrible, as if a dozen iron spears were being hammered against the door.

"Quickly!" I urged, because the Irishman showed no sense of urgency.

"Little lady," he murmured, still hanging back, "I'm sure this is a mistake. I can't think of any reason under

11

Heaven why these men should be after *me*. No-one even knows me here –"

"Never mind reasons!" I almost screamed at him. "People in these parts are brilliant at inventing excuses for violence if it suits them."

Somehow I got him into the dairy, through the trap-door and down the steep mud steps to the airless little room. I showed him a sort of bench beside the last stocks of winter's meat: he brushed aside the cobwebs and sat down.

"You'll be all right here in the dark?" I asked, starting alone up the steps again with the lamp.

"I have no fear of anything."

I hurried back to the hall. The whole household was huddled at the far end, watching Uncle Egil as, with trembling hands, he once more pulled back the bolt of the great door.

Outside, a rough voice barked: "Open up! The chieftains' orders are to search every single farm in the district – and to burn down the houses of any who try to stop us!"

Then the door was thrown open and they came stamping in on us – twenty massive, beefy men in armour. The dim, yellowish light from the whale-oil burners showed up ugly fighting scars on their faces, and thick veins rippling in the hairy hands that clasped their weapons.

"Who calls himself the master of this house?" The one who spoke looked the mightiest of them all. His red beard and bushy eyebrows were as thick as fox fur. The

12

floor seemed to shudder under his step.

"Egil Olafsson at your service," said my uncle, coming forward politely. "And, er . . . you are welcome to come in, and enjoy the humble hospitality of my house."

Old red-beard relaxed a little. "That's a fair enough greeting, Egil," he rasped. "I'm Grim Helgisson – leader of this band of men."

"And, er, what is your business, Grim?" enquired Uncle Egil.

"Our business is chasing evil out of this land, of course!" cried Grim, getting all frothed up again. "Rampant evil!"

"I can assure you there's no evil in *my* house," said Uncle Egil quietly. "You may have heard my history, Grim? But then perhaps you haven't. In my youth I went out raiding and a-viking with the best of them. Oho, there was a time when I'd have had a lesson to teach even to a great man like you! But all I ever gained from it was trouble and grief, and the loss of my dearest brother. So I've steered clear of such goings-on for the last ten years. I'm well known around here for the quiet and private way I live."

"Aha," retorted Grim, "but it's not you I'm accusing, host. Perhaps you keep too much to your own four walls and fields to know about the man we're after." He spat disgustedly onto the floor. "Man? – it's a disgrace to call him a man! He's a sorcerer! A maker of black magic, a caster of evil spells!"

I clutched at Aunt Thorhalla's hand, and a ripple of shock ran like a breeze through the listening servants.

"I suppose, being all shut away here," Grim went on impatiently, "that you've heard nothing of the wretchedness that's been sweeping across the country, from one valley to the next? You don't know about all the babies that have died, eh? Or the hundreds of sheep sickening and wasting away?"

He lowered his red, shaggy head to peer closely at my uncle, as if trying to decide whether such worldly ignorance could possibly be genuine.

"Odin All-Father protect us!" exclaimed Aunt Thorhalla. "I had no idea things were as bad as that! A sorcerer – round here? Tell us, Grim: what kind of man is this villain?"

"He is an alien, madam," replied Grim, short and sharp and crisp.

"An alien?"

"A foreigner. One who speaks in strange accents and outlandish tongues."

Uncle Egil paled.

"His victims have been bringing their grievances to the law courts," continued Grim, "and the chieftains have ruled that the evil must be hunted down. When we find him, we'll squash the insect out – like this!" With his heel he ground his own spittle into the rushes spread across the floor. "So we're searching every house and every farm, one by one, because, by Thor, he must be hiding *somewhere* so long as winter grips the land."

For a horrible moment I thought that someone would lose their head and give the game away about Ruadh – most likely Kjartan, whom for my part I never would trust at all.

But before anyone else could dare to speak, Uncle Egil shrugged resignedly and said, "Search as you wish, Grim: we've nothing and no-one worth hiding."

Aunt Thorhalla clapped her hands at the servants to bring food and ale for our visitors, as he continued:

"This is my foster daughter, Ingrid. She'll be glad to show you around."

He must have thought that Grim would have more faith in a girl, but I stared at my uncle in numb disbelief. My heart began to pound and I could scarcely swallow. The other men were already making themselves at home around the fire, and there was no way out of it: I led the great, gruff fellow on his way.

It was a ghastly task. I had to take him round every inch of the house and wait while he peered under benches, poked into chests and closets and tapped the wooden panelling with a horny thumbnail to see if it were hollow. I did my best to keep at a distance: his smell – of old leather, alcohol and sweat – made me feel thick-headed and sick.

Eventually we came to the dairy door and Grim pushed me in ahead of him. I stood back and held my breath while he lifted the lid off each of the great vats of curds and milk, and sniffed suspiciously inside. I prayed with all my heart that Ruadh would keep still.

Then Grim spied a sack of flour that might have been just big enough to hide a man; and as he crossed the room, his eye fell upon the trap-door that lay in the floor before it.

At the same time there came a rustling, a sound of

15

something moving.

He froze at once and listened, turning his head like a dog on the alert.

"What's that?"

Again we heard it: a sound like a hand clawing over fabric.

He crossed towards the flour-sack, hesitating suspiciously to listen by the trap-door. Then, all at once he leaped forward and, with a single, sweeping stroke, slashed the sack clean in two with his sword.

The pale grain poured silently out into a heap upon the floor. I jumped back in alarm – and then, as if the gods had sent it, a tiny mouse suddenly scurried out and ran helter-skelter for its life across the room!

Grim forgot the trap-door, he even forgot his search for a moment, as he threw back his shaggy head and laughed. A good, hearty laugh it was – a gurgling roar from deep in the throat. When he was finished, he thumped me cheerily on the back like an old friend. Then, still chuckling, he strode back to the main hall to join his men at their ale and feasting.

"Why host, don't you dare tell me again there's no evil in this house!" he cried delightedly. "Evil, man? Just take a look in your store-room. There's a horde of hungry mice there, eating you out of house and home!"

His men, who had been swigging back our best ale as freely as water, almost laughed themselves off the benches. We did our best to join in, though all poor Uncle Egil could manage, perched uncomfortably on his high-seat, was a watery smile.

Several of the men had thrown off their cloaks and loosened their belts, glancing longingly at the neat rolls of quilts and bed-rugs piled up against the walls.

But Grim grabbed a huge mug of ale from the table and emptied it in a single draught.

"Come on, lads," he roared at them, "there's hunting to be done! Once the snows melt, the Sorcerer could easily slip from our clutches." He patted his rounded, leather-clad belly and stuffed a whole griddle-cake into his mouth. "You've served us well, host, but I'm afraid we can't accept your good offer of a bed."

"Such a shame," murmured Aunt Thorhalla, watching with relief as the men, belching and bellowing, fastened their armour and took up their axes, spears and swords.

Out through the great door they rushed, into the frosty air with their breath steaming like geysers, throwing themselves onto their horses to gallop off down the road towards the hills.

As I watched, the scene became imprinted on my mind like some vision from a war myth; but then I felt my uncle's touch on my shoulder, drawing me inside.

He slid the bolt across the door and beckoned us to join him at the fire so that we might draw some comfort from its warmth.

CHAPTER 2

Send him Away!

Down in the dark, cramped earth-house, the flickering beam of my lamp showed Ruadh kneeling with his back to the steps. His hands were clasped before him, and he was muttering mysterious words in a lilting rhythm under his breath.

I thought at once of spells and incantations: a shiver inched up my spine and my legs turned weak as porridge.

He was so absorbed in his secret business that he did not even notice my approach.

"They've gone, Ruadh," I said, trying to keep my voice

steady. "You can come out now."

He turned round and slowly stood up, flinching at the unaccustomed light.

"That was a short visit," he remarked, his calmness soothing my fear of him. In his underground cell, he could have heard nothing of what had passed.

He followed me back up to the dairy. I made sure of seeing how his face reacted when I said, "It *was* you they wanted."

"Me? Oh no, little lady, I don't think so."

Not a shadow flickered across his warm eyes.

Uncle Egil and Aunt Thorhalla were standing side by side in the hall. Extra lamps had been lit, and the fire stoked up into a brilliant yellow blaze. The servants were busy clearing away the sorry remains of the feast; but I could see Kjartan lurking furtively behind a pillar at the far end of the room.

Uncle Egil said shortly, "They tell me you're a sorcerer, Irishman. You're a doomed man."

Ruadh blinked at him. "They tell you . . .?" he repeated politely.

"Look here, foreigner," Aunt Thorhalla interrupted, "we've taken you in and kept you hidden, haven't we – at the risk of having our house burnt down! So don't you dare try any of your black magic on us!"

"Black magic?" The charge sank in at last: his fists clenched and his serene features exploded into life. "You take me for . . ." he stumbled over the words, ". . . for a *wizard*? But it's unthinkable! My friends, we Irish are Christians –"

19

"Ah, so that's the nonsense you mix yourself in!" cried my aunt. "Just you remember this: we worship Thor and Odin in this country, stranger! There's been enough fools trying to turn us from our gods these last few years – most likely, half of them were sorcerers like you. Now – take your wickedness and be off at once!"

Ruadh looked so hurt that my heart went out to him. Before I could stop myself, I blurted out: "I don't believe he *is* the Sorcerer!"

Aunt Thorhalla's voice turned shrill with terror: "Oh, just hear what madness the child speaks! She's already under your power!"

I tried to protest, to explain myself, but she would not hear me.

"Egil, get rid of him! Be quick and send the wretch away!"

"Let's have no trouble," said Uncle Egil. "Will you go quietly?"

Ruadh shrugged and fetched his damp cloak from the corner where it lay. "I dare say you mean for the best," he murmured, "though your customs seem strange to my way of thinking. This would never happen in Ireland."

Uncle Egil caught sight of Kjartan hovering in the shadows. "Slave boy," he called, "what are you doing there? Make yourself useful. Walk with this . . . man to the edge of the home-field and see him briskly on his road."

He opened the door and Kjartan, flinging a rough cloak across his shoulders, led the Irishman out into the frost. He met my gaze with a smirk of triumph, leaving me with an inexplicable sense of loss.

"That boy!" I cried when they were gone. "He's ruder and lazier than anyone!"

"He was bought as a bargain," said Uncle Egil. "But his muscles are strong."

"At least we can be sure he'll take the Sorcerer as far as we've sent him," said Aunt Thorhalla. "As like as not, he'll see which way he's heading, too – I've never known a slave with such a passion for spying." She turned to me with a look of pity. "My dear, you've seen too much for one night. It's time you went to bed."

"But first you must pray to wise Odin to save you from the foreigner's wicked magic," said Uncle Egil, kissing me goodnight with real feeling. "Oh, pray to him hard, poor Ingrid!"

I woke with a start at the sound of something banging outside. Could it be Grim and his beery men come back?

I lay still and listened.

Through the thick turf walls I could hear the wind groaning through the valley. I realised that the banging was only a bucket or some iron farm implement being blown about in the yard.

I turned over and tried to sleep.

But it was as if the wind had caught me up in its tumbling, making me restless and wide awake. I thought

21

of Ruadh and wondered what protection his worn cloak would be against the bitter springtime gales.

At last, on an impulse to help him, I climbed out of bed in the darkness, pulled on my clothes and crept across the hall.

Everything was quiet inside, except for the snores of the servants sleeping on the benches. The fire had died into a soft, red glow of embers. I felt around the hearthstones and found a couple of slabs of cold bread. They would be better than nothing for a man who was starving.

Clutching them tightly, I came to the door and felt for the great iron bolt, trying to pull it back. It was heavy, far too heavy: my fingers scraped and stumbled helplessly over the cold, hard metal.

Suddenly, I heard someone behind me. I whirled round so violently that my loose hair went flying and slashed across the other's face.

By the light of a small candle that he shielded with his cupped hand, I saw Kjartan.

"What's the matter, young Mistress?"

I took a deep breath to steady myself.

"Open the door for me since you're here," I whispered as haughtily as I could.

He made no move.

"Please open the door for me."

"Where are you going?" he asked slyly. He knew he had me cornered: I would get into as much trouble as he for wandering around at this time of night. I dared not strike him or make a fuss, for fear of waking my uncle and aunt.

"Don't ask questions, slave boy. Do as you're told."

He edged round to block my way and stared at me full on.

"You're going to follow the Irishman, aren't you?" he said tauntingly.

He played teasingly with the bolt. My uncle was right: he was strong. He pulled back the great iron bar as easily as a feather; and then at once rammed it shut again.

"That's an odd thing for a high-born young lady to do," he said, imitating the way that Aunt Thorhalla spoke. He even had the cheek to wave a reprimanding finger at me. "Off in the night after a foreign sorcerer, eh? Whatever would your foster parents think of that – Ingrid?"

He wasn't ever supposed to address us by our proper names: it was the height of impudence.

"Open the door at once, you nasty little slave," I hissed. "Then go away – and mind your own business."

"Don't call me that," he snarled back. "I'm too good to be a slave. Better than you are." He grasped my arm so hard that I winced. "Give me my freedom, Ingrid."

"Don't be stupid, how can I?" I said, slapping him away. "And why should I want to? Just wait till the morning – I'll see that you're whipped!"

"But what about you?" he said. "Creeping up in the night like a thief, eh?" He stared pointedly at the bread in my hand. "Taking food to an outlaw who's condemned to death. What will happen when they hear about *that*?"

We glared hatefully at each other in the flickering candlelight, while the silence grew into a stony wall between us. At last, to break the tension, I said, "Anyway, I don't believe he *is* the Sorcerer."

23

To my surprise, Kjartan softened at once.

"No," he said. And then, "I wondered, when you said it before, whether you really meant it."

He slid back the bolt and stepped politely aside. "If you like, I'll tell you which way he went."

"But . . . why?"

"Your people should never have sent him away like that," he said. "He told me he's been really ill. He badly needs help. He hasn't got a single friend in Iceland." He cleared his throat. "He's gone south – along Trout River, heading towards the Smoky Mountains."

I swung open the door just far enough to stare out at the night. The wind came tearing and whistling down under a full moon, skimming over the ice.

"If you go after him on horseback," said Kjartan behind me, "you're bound to catch him up soon."

It was ridiculous, foolhardy . . . But Ruadh's sad smile and his hopeless quest loomed hauntingly in my mind's eye. Supposing he could find no shelter? It would be our fault if he died out there, all alone in the wilderness.

"If you dare tell a soul what I'm doing," I said fiercely, "I really will have you flogged!" But when I looked round, Kjartan was gone.

I shrugged and stepped out into the night.

Half-way across the yard, footsteps came running after me.

"Mistress Ingrid – take this!" Kjartan grabbed my hand, prised open the fingers and thrust into it a short sword in a leather scabbard. So, I thought, a thief too! Judging by his speed he must be in the habit of helping himself to things from Uncle Egil's weapon store.

I was all ready to flare up at him again. But he said warningly, "You might need it. There's others on the road tonight beside our friend Ruadh."

All too late, I remembered Grim and his merry band. But I couldn't turn back and lose face now – not in front of a slave.

I grunted a sort of thank you, and stamped on through the snow to the stables. Kjartan shadowed me.

"Ingrid . . ."

"What now?" I hissed furiously.

"Good luck," he whispered. And then I heard him retreating softly towards the house.

CHAPTER 3

The Prophecy

Inside the warm, straw-bedded stables I called my favourite pony, Ice Star, gently by her name. She padded across to nuzzle me and came outside without a murmur, though her breath billowed into huge clouds of steam with the cold.

We crept quiet as ghosts out of the farm, past the turf-roofed sheep sheds and the snow-blanketed pastures. The moon and stars reflected on the ice to give a good light, though clouds kept scudding across and casting eerie shadows.

I had to slip to the ground to examine the vague tracks where the valley road began. It was just possible to make out Ruadh's footprints, heading southward through the snow.

At length, as we followed his lonely trail, the moon began to fade and streaks of yellow and crimson seeped into the eastern sky. It was turning less cold. Ice Star quickened her pace a little.

In the strengthening light, perhaps a quarter of a mile ahead, suddenly there was a figure walking slowly, back bent against the groaning wind, wrapped from head to heel in a misshapen sheepskin cloak.

I urged Ice Star onwards. But as we drew closer, the wind rose and swept the noise of our coming away from the walker.

I called out, "Ruadh!" but this too blew back at me and he did not turn.

At last I drew almost level with the grey-clad figure and called his name again. In the middle of a step he stopped short in surprise.

He did not speak, but merely looked at me as I dismounted, his face shadowed under his deep hood.

"What do you want with me?" he said at last. I caught a curious accent, but there was something wrong with his voice: it was thin and irritable, not at all as I remembered it.

"Ruadh, it's me, Ingrid, you remember? I'm so sorry we sent you away like that last night . . . Only, you see, my uncle's been a nervous man ever since . . . anyway, Kjartan told me you need help, so I . . ."

He swallowed my apologies with a laugh, but it contained none of the patient good humour I remembered him by. I searched under the folds of his vast cowl for some glimpse of those reassuringly warm eyes, but with his back to the growing light, I could see nothing.

"Ha!" he cried, "so you've come to help *me*, girl?" He threw back his hood, and I saw to my horror that it was not Ruadh at all.

He was of the same build and colouring, he spoke with a similar lilting accent, but there the likeness ended. For this man had eyes as hollow as a chasm, and his dark beard was wispy and pointed like a goat's.

I stood there blinking at him, while the sun came up to flood the distant mountains with golden light. My right hand tightened over the sword that hung in its scabbard at my hip. I saw his pale lips curl back again into that joyless laugh.

"Who are you?" I said foolishly.

"Surely," he said, "*surely* you know me?"

I edged back towards Ice Star. "I'm sorry, I thought you were . . . I was looking for someone else."

"But you've found me now," he cried, all at once seizing my sword-arm in an iron hold. "There's plenty of others would be glad enough to catch up with me. I've heard rumours that half the district's out looking for me."

My mouth went dry, the blood throbbed furiously in my head. His grip burned into my skin. I tried to ease the sword into the other hand behind my back, but he stopped me with a word.

"That won't help you," he hissed. "A sword is useless against my power!"

I waited: there was no deafening clap of thunder, no shaking of the earth to fanfare our meeting.

"Are you . . . the Sorcerer?" I whispered at last.

He nodded, and flicked my wrist free; but under his bottomless gaze I still felt pinned down and trapped.

"Who were you looking for?"

It was useless to fight against his will: as if a knife were at my throat, he drew the words from me. "A friend . . . an Irishman. A foreigner like yourself, sir."

"So – you mistake me for a fool from the green hills of Ireland, eh? That land of drivelling Christian saints! Well, get this right, girl: *I* come from a sinful corner of the Earth. It's a place so storm-swept that nothing will grow there and the sheep must live on seaweed. I can tell you, after a while I got tired of rooting like a bird among the stones, scavenging for food." He lowered his voice. "I have my dignity to think of. That's why I turned to wizardry, to keep myself alive."

I stared at my feet: as the day warmed up, the snow was starting to melt around them. Down in the valley bottom I could hear the river creaking out of its covering of ice.

"I suppose a nice girl like you would be surprised to know," he went on, "that out in the big, wide world there are plenty of spiteful people willing to pay a sorcerer well if he proves his skill at poisoning their neighbours' sheep, and spreading sickness in their enemies' families."

He paused, watching my face.

"But," I said nervously, "but . . . now you've come to

29

live here in Iceland, sir, you can surely see that there's enough good land for everyone to get enough food. Surely, sir, you don't *need* your magic here?"

"Ha!" he mocked, "but I've sold my whole soul to evil now, haven't I, eh? There's no escaping from that. There's only one way I'm capable of living now – and that's by selling my dark spells. I'm trapped by what I am, girl!"

I could scarcely bring myself to speak in reply, but he prodded me and hissed, "Tell me, what do you think of me now?"

"I . . . I sort of feel sorry for you," I mumbled.

He seemed satisfied. "Then you can go . . ."

I turned to find Ice Star, but she had wandered uneasily back down the road.

" . . . Wait!" he snapped. "I haven't finished with you yet. You can go when you've told me everything I need to know."

He was lean and hungry like a crow.

"What . . . what do you want to know?" I whispered, still trying to edge away.

"Have you seen the men who are after me?"

I hesitated.

He came closer. "Tell me!"

"Yes . . ."

"How many of them are there?"

"About . . . twenty, I think."

"Their names?"

I feared he would set his spells on them if he knew who they were: even fiery Grim did not deserve that.

"I don't know," I said.

He let out a weird, muted shriek of impatience. "Come, girl, tell me their names!"

I felt his will setting itself, rock-hard, against my own.

"I can't!" I said, and did not give in.

"Aach! No matter. What did they say?"

"Nothing much. That . . . that you were outlawed and they were hunting you down. They searched our house."

"And what did they find? Your Irish friend?"

"No," I said, "nothing. We hid him and then sent him on his way at once – thinking he was you."

He laughed at that and seemed relieved. "And where did these . . . hunters go after that? Are they on my track?"

"I don't think so," I said.

He looked at me long and hard. A short distance away, Ice Star scraped at the slushy snow with her hoof and whinnied to be on her way.

"It's a long time since anyone was ever straight with me," he said. "Come, you've given me a few minutes' rare company – let me do something for you in return. Give me your palm and I'll read your fortune from it."

I shuddered to let him take my hand in his bony fingers and hold it up to scrutiny; besides, I preferred not to know what twists and turns my future held. But I did not dare to refuse. He took an age to reach his verdict: the sun rose high and strong, turning the snow to water before my very eyes.

"Firstly," he said, "I see we're to meet again." My heart sank. "But no more of that. Now, here's your destiny, girl:

31

one day, the humblest of men shall be your lord."

He dropped my hand abruptly and I waited in puzzlement.

"You look as if you think it's a curse," he said, "but it may turn out to be a blessing. There, now go."

He pulled the hood back over his angular head, and turned again to the south.

Now it was I who delayed. "Just a minute, what do you mean? I don't understand!"

"Simpleton!" he cried. "Get back to your farm. And I warn you," he added, facing me full on again, "don't you dare hint to a single soul that you've met me. My spells can travel a hundred miles if necessary."

Then he was off without a backward glance, strutting towards the distant mountains, sending up glistening showers of snow-melt with every step he took.

CHAPTER 4

Rumours

Uncle Egil looked resplendent in his smartest clothes. He was setting off for the Great Assembly, to sell the cloth my aunt had woven, and to hear all Iceland's business and gossip. The horses were saddled and laden with wares and provisions.

In the early summer sunshine, Aunt Thorhalla was clucking around him like an old mother hen: "I don't know, Egil, as if I didn't spend all last winter at the weaving loom – yet you still complain there's not enough for your trading. I've loaded up ten fat bales of cloth –

33

what more do you want? Don't tell me that's not enough to keep us in flour and ale for the next year!"

"It's our little Ingrid, though," said Uncle Egil, smiling at me sheepishly as he polished his most expensive sword with a soft piece of kid-skin. "You see, dearest, she's made a special request. Just a small one, mind, but of course I'd like to try and help her if I can."

"Well, Ingrid, what is it?"

"I've asked if Uncle might perhaps do a little business for me after the Great Assembly," I began.

"Business!" exploded Aunt Thorhalla. "We're farmers, not professional traders! Whatever is this about?"

"It's . . . the slaves," I said. "It's just that I thought perhaps Uncle could arrange an exchange."

"You're stepping a bit above yourself, aren't you?" said my aunt. She took her spinning from the pocket of her apron and set the spindle to twirl furiously as she spoke. "Wait till you come into your inheritance and you're mistress of your own house – that's the time to start worrying about slaves!"

"But you *have* been worrying, haven't you?" said Uncle Egil, sticking up for me as usual.

"It's that boy," I explained.

"Kjartan?" said Aunt Thorhalla. "Well, he's strong enough and does the work we set him, doesn't he?"

"He pesters her," said Uncle Egil.

But Aunt Thorhalla never was a woman to stand for any nonsense. "Pshaw! Box his ears, Ingrid, and send him on his way! Were you thinking of selling him then, Egil? Would he fetch a good price?"

"Not very," said Uncle Egil. "I don't know his breeding, you see. And besides, word seems to have got around, from people who have been our house guests, that he's an insolent fellow. I'm afraid he would cost me something to replace."

"Well, that's all the cloth we've got," said Aunt Thorhalla, "so if it'll buy no more than provisions, you'll just have to learn to live with the wretch, Ingrid, and that's that. Now hurry along, Egil, you always dither so. Where are you meeting your relations? By the ford? It won't do to be late, with the long ride ahead of you."

"I wish I could come," I said, as we went to see him on his way.

"Next summer perhaps . . ." suggested my uncle.

"Oh, don't encourage her!" exclaimed my aunt. "A girl who's to have her own farm one day had best spend her time at home learning how to manage it. There'll be time enough to attend Assemblies when you know more what you're about, my girl. Now, goodbye dearest, travel safely, mind you get some bargains, and be sure to bring us home plenty of news!"

She pecked him fondly on the cheek. Then, with a quick wave of her ever-busy hand, she bustled me back indoors.

We went into the dairy to see how the women were getting on with the cheese and butter making. They needed more milk and my aunt sent me out to fetch it. As I went, Kjartan happened to go past, bowed down and cursing under a huge sack of newly shorn wool.

I turned my back on him at once; but he hovered in the doorway.

"You haven't forgotten?" he hissed.

I ignored him.

"Ruadh." He spoke the name shortly and sharply, guessing its effect. "It's more than two months since your people sent him off into the mountains. Do you think he's survived?"

"Go away, slave."

"Why won't you tell me whether you found him that night?"

"I'll tell you nothing."

Not a word, the Sorcerer had said, not a word to anyone. How could I possibly risk his anger, just to satisfy a slave boy's prying?

"I've asked my uncle to sell you," I said.

He shrugged and almost dropped his bundles.

"You're keeping things from me, Mistress Ingrid . . ." I was about to strike him, when he added, "and I'm keeping things from you too!" before scurrying away.

Many of the travellers on their way to the Great Assembly stopped at our house, seeking food and a bed for the night, so we were kept busy for the next few days. They brought us word of all the latest weddings and feuds, which was good payment for our hospitality. Only this year there seemed more sad news than usual, as the foul breath of wizardry spread across the land.

When the last of the travellers had ridden onwards, some other folk came knocking.

There were three of them: ragged, wrinkled beggar women, such as you often see wandering through the farmlands – women whom fortune has not treated kindly, and who live by selling gossip for a crust of bread and a warm place to sleep.

Aunt Thorhalla let them in and sat them down by the open door.

"Thank you for your welcome, lady," said the scraggiest of the three. "Now, our names are Groa, Helga and Vigdis, and we've got a great deal to tell, if you'll hear us out."

The other two nodded their grey, wrinkled heads vigorously and chewed on their toothless gums.

"We're always glad to hear something new," said my aunt. "But remember, there's been plenty of others stopping here before you, so don't go telling us what we've already heard."

Groa cleared her throat noisily and straightened herself on the bench. She had soft, rosy cheeks and a ready smile: beneath her weather-worn skin you could see that once she must have been quite a dazzling beauty.

"He is still free!" she began dramatically. "Not even the gods can stop him!"

"Who's free?" I asked.

"It's the Sorcerer she's talking about," said Vigdis, "isn't it, Groa dear? She really ought to explain herself more precisely," she whispered to Helga, "folks want to hear a story that starts from the beginning and goes on to the end."

37

"The Sorcerer is free," continued Groa, "and no-one can catch him. But there's many who've been taken in by him, to their shame! He's been glimpsed all over the place – yet no-one will ever own up that they know where he is. I tell you, lady, we've been to houses where whole families swear that they've never been near him – but *we* know better than that, don't we, sisters?"

"We surely do," agreed Helga. "We can smell it in the air when the evil one's around."

I got up and stood in the shadow of the doorway, lest they should see me blushing.

"There can't be many would shelter him, knowing what he is," said Aunt Thorhalla cautiously. "But is it true: have they really not caught up with the villain yet?"

"It's those whose babies are sick that I feel sorriest for," said Helga, shaking her head at my aunt. "The cattle and sheep dying – well, it happens. But it's a sad thing when a woman in the flush of youth can't produce a healthy child."

"Oh, but sister," cried Vigdis suddenly, prodding Groa in her excitement, "you haven't told them everything yet! You've forgotten the most important part."

"Indeed, that's right," said Groa. She gave Aunt Thorhalla a sly, sideways look. "Did you know, lady, that the Sorcerer has been spotted along this very road?"

"*This* road?" said Aunt Thorhalla.

"Yes! And who do you think saw him?"

My aunt shook her head, her face clouding.

"It was us! We saw him with our own eyes!"

"Strolling along, if you please – and never mind that

the snow lay thick on the ground," said Helga.

My aunt gazed very hard out through the door, her mouth set into an inscrutable blank. "To think he's been so near . . ."

"There's more to it than that, though," Groa went on. "Here's a bit of news about your own farm, lady, that perhaps you'd rather not hear; but let's hope you'll at least thank us for telling you."

She cleared her throat. "Not long after the Sorcerer passed this way, someone else was seen, riding hard after him – from your very own stables!"

"Following the villain," cried Helga, "though it's hard to believe."

My aunt looked at me nervously, and I was gladder than ever that the shadows hid my burning cheeks.

"Ingrid, whoever . . .?" For a moment, I thought she half suspected me; the hags were clearly waiting for an answer, and in panic I blurted out:

"It *must* have been Kjartan! He was sent to take him on his way . . ." All too late I realised what I was saying, and my hand flew to my mouth. ". . . He took . . . that guest we had on his way," I finished feebly.

There was an awful silence. Then Aunt Thorhalla said quietly, "Ingrid, would you go and fetch these ladies some more to eat, please."

I went out obediently, and in due course the three went on their way.

As soon as they had gone, Aunt Thorhalla set to scolding me: "Oh, you hopeless, foolish child! There's so many bad folk hungering after trouble just now: can't you learn when to hold your tongue?"

I'd have given anything to take back those words. An uneasy foreboding hung over us. Then, a few mornings later as I crossed the yard, a heavy brown horse came cantering in. Leering down at me like an overgrown troll in the saddle sat Grim Helgisson.

"Young Ingrid – remember me?"

I was shaking like butter in the churning, but I managed to look him full in the eye.

"I . . . think so."

He dismounted and strode across, pushing long, stray locks of flaming hair out of his face with a huge, grimy hand.

"Where's your foster father?"

"At the Great Assembly, sir."

It was a needless question: every free man whose body will carry him goes to the main event of the year.

"The Assembly's over," said Grim shortly, stamping with impatience. "I've just come from there myself. Isn't he back yet?"

"No sir, he –"

"Where is he?" He spat the words out before I could finish.

"He . . . I think he had business to do on his way back. He was going to the Fjords to do some trading."

"Thor's thunder! Have I missed him?" He stood dead still, towering above me, flushing with silent anger until I thought that he would burst.

Over his shoulder, I suddenly noticed a small group of armed men waiting on the other side of the home-field.

Whatever did they want with Uncle Egil?

"Shall I fetch my aunt?" I offered.

Grim's full lips worked soundlessly for a moment under the bristling moustache; and then all at once he swung his large frame back onto the horse to loom over me, more threatening than ever.

"It's your foster father I want."

"But – why, sir?"

"He is a liar and a public enemy! He hid an outlaw under this roof of yours on the very night we came to hunt the villain down. Within an hour of our leaving here, the Sorcerer was seen setting straight out from this farm. He knowingly helped the most despicable of criminals – to the shame of every honest man and woman in Iceland, whose blood cries out for revenge!"

"Not Uncle Egil! Not my foster father!" But Grim glowered through my protests, as if I were no more than a transparent fragment of his dreams.

"I came here to kill him," he said, his voice soft as a flame licking at the log it will soon devour. "Today then, he's escaped with his life. He's lucky. But tell him –"

"In Thor's name, I beg you to have pity!" I cried. For a brief moment he hesitated, and a look almost of sorrow crossed his face, though it passed in a flash.

"Tell him I shall be back."

He pulled out his sword with a strange, half-choked roar and pointed it for a moment full at my throat.

"The law is the law," he said. "A man must take what's due to him – if there's to be any justice in the land!"

CHAPTER 5

The Dream

Two days later, horse hooves came clattering again into the yard. We dropped our work and rushed out to find Uncle Egil, looking as pleased as a ram in springtime. He was beaming from ear to ear and busily unloading bags and packages from the ponies.

"Oh, my dear husband!" cried Aunt Thorhalla, rushing up to fling her arms about him. "Is it really you? Alive and safe and unharmed?"

"Goodness me," he chuckled as he freed himself from her. "What's the matter? I'm not used to such affection,

dear Thorhalla! It makes me feel quite young again . . ."
he winked at me ". . . especially as there's so much talk in
the air of weddings."

"Weddings!" we echoed together, forgetting all our
worries for a moment at one thought of such delicious
gossip. "Whose?"

But he would not tell us another snippet until he had
finished his unpacking. Then we carried benches outside
into the sunshine and settled ourselves by the stream at
the bottom of the home-field, where the banks were all
purple with arctic fireweed.

"Presents first," said Uncle Egil, handing us each a
small parcel wrapped in scarlet cloth. For my aunt there
was a pair of filigree brooches, all gleaming coils, knots
and fine interlacings; whilst to me he gave a tiny gold
Thor's Hammer on a twisted golden chain to wear
around my neck.

I held the pendant in the palm of my hand. It glinted
softly dull with hidden fires in the clear summer light.

"You must wear it always to bring you luck," my uncle
said; and there was something in his voice that sent a
brief shiver down my spine.

Aunt Thorhalla pinned the new brooches to her dress
and then went twirling around the meadow in them, so
that my uncle looked more pleased with himself than
ever.

"There'll be plenty of dancing in a few weeks," he
laughed.

My aunt came tripping back, and we both begged to be
told whose wedding was in the offing.

"It's Ingrid's first cousin Gudrun," he announced solemnly, "daughter of my youngest brother Snorri." We laughed with gladness at the news: Gudrun was always so plump and lazy and getting into silly scrapes that no-one ever thought she'd win a husband for herself.

"Who's to be the lucky man?" asked Aunt Thorhalla.

"Well now – guess," said Uncle Egil, looking unaccountably mischievous.

We recited the names of all the unmarried men we knew in the district.

"It's none of them!" he cried delightedly. "It's a lad named Mord. Now, whose son do you think he is?"

"Oh, hurry up and tell us everything, for goodness sake!"

"He's the son of Grim!" said Uncle Egil.

"Of Grim . . . ?"

"Yes, Grim Helgisson, the very same who came hunting after that mad Irishman we hid at the end of last winter. Can you imagine – we're to be joined to *that* ruffian by marriage!"

My aunt and I looked at each other.

"Does Grim know about the wedding?"

"No, more's the pity. Apparently, as soon as Snorri had given his blessing to the happy couple, the lad went hurrying to his father's tent to tell him – only to find that Grim had left the Great Assembly early, on urgent business – a feud, so they said. Meanwhile, this poor lad Mord is head over heels in love – can you imagine – with Gudrun!"

He laughed again, but we did not join in this time. "What's the matter?" he asked.

I told him about Grim's recent visit and his threats. But to our consternation, Uncle Egil was in such good spirits that at first the danger he was in did not seem to sink in.

"He'd come to *kill* you, Uncle," I said again.

But on that warm afternoon, with the insects buzzing dreamily, the birds twittering in the blue sky and the stream singing past our feet, it was hard to take the thought of death seriously.

"Well, I dare say old Grim is home by now," said Uncle Egil lightly, "and his son Mord will have told him that our families are to be united. So now he'll probably drop his case against me altogether, or at least settle it in some other way. Well, well, what a state of affairs! Whoever could have told Grim such tales?"

"I bet Kjartan had something to do with it," I said quickly. "You didn't manage to sell him, Uncle, did you?"

"I'm afraid not," he said, "though I did try. I even had one or two offers; but when it came to it, no-one would give me a good enough price."

"I wish you'd got rid of him anyway," I said crossly.

"I bought you presents instead," said Uncle Egil gently. "Now, let's not argue, because I'm afraid I have to leave you again tomorrow. I've promised to call on Snorri to help prepare for cousin Gudrun's wedding; and after all this trouble with Mord's father, I've half a mind to show my good intentions by offering to hold it here. What do you think, dearest?"

"I'm all for it, if it'll help to keep the head on your shoulders," said Aunt Thorhalla, "though I shudder to think of the expense. But as for your going off to arrange it all – is it wise to travel when Grim's warned us that he's after your life?"

"Oh, what a flap about nothing!" cried Uncle Egil. "I've told you, Thorhalla, he won't be after me now."

"But with all this suspicion, and the Sorcerer still on the loose! Just supposing –"

"Dear dear, supposing, supposing . . . Come, let me see you dancing again in your new brooches, Thorhalla. Aren't you pleased to have me home?"

Out of the night, a dreadful scream forced my eyes open.

I sat bolt upright in bed, rigid and listening, until I realised that it was my own piercing voice that I had heard.

Aunt Thorhalla came running, Uncle Egil at her heels, bringing candles and comfort.

"Ingrid, hush, hush, what's wrong? Have you been dreaming?"

I nodded, blinking at the dancing, imp-like shadows that the flickering candle flame made. I felt cold and weak, sore with irrational terror.

They sat down on the end of my bed and made me tell them what it was about.

"There was a swan," I began, "flying alone across the sky. Then suddenly some ravens appeared – huge black things, making a great dark cloud."

"But why are you trembling, Ingrid?" said Uncle Egil.

"The ravens started croaking and screeching. They mobbed the swan – attacked it – until at last there was a dreadful silence and they flew away. Then, where the swan had been there was nothing . . . except two tear-shaped drops of blood. That's when I woke up – as you found me."

"Well, that's a dream to mull over, to be sure," said my aunt, plumping up the pillow for me and smoothing out the eider-feather quilt. "What can it mean?"

Uncle Egil shrugged. "Some kind of bad luck, it would seem." He gave a little chuckle, but I could tell it was only meant to reassure me. "Well, whatever it is, we can talk about it in the morning before I leave. Go back to sleep now, Ingrid."

But I could not rest, turning one moment hot and the next one cold. They brought me water and extra sheepskins, but nothing was enough.

"Come now," said my aunt, stifling a yawn, "what do you want? We can't stay up all night."

"I *must* know what it means," I said. "Now. Please."

"Well," she sighed, "if the child has such a feeling, we'd be foolish to ignore it. You'd better wake the whole household, Egil, and see if anyone's got enough insight to offer a clue. I'm completely baffled by it."

So all the slaves and servants were called from their beds and told about my dream. One by one they shook their bleary-eyed heads.

Until it came to Kjartan.

He waited, patient and alert, for his turn to be

questioned; and then he said at once: "Master, I believe I know what it means. The swan is surely yourself."

Uncle Egil paled. "You think so, boy? What about the ravens?"

Kjartan wriggled his bare toes on the cold, earthen floor. "They may be a gang of men waiting for you – in an ambush." He hesitated. "The dream tells what'll happen if you let yourself be trapped. Perhaps . . . perhaps the drops of blood are my Mistress Thorhalla and" (he stared at me) "young Mistress Ingrid."

"I see," said Uncle Egil. There was a long silence.

"This is almost more than I can bear," whispered Aunt Thorhalla, suddenly weak as a puppy. It was so unlike her that I felt a new flood of fear.

"Those are bold words that you've spoken, slave-boy," said Uncle Egil. His voice rang out oddly. "Let's see whether you're right." He called two of the most trusted manservants, "Lambi, and you, Bolli, ride out at once along the road I'll be taking later to my brother Snorri's house, and see if you meet anyone along the way."

He turned to comfort my aunt, though the hand that took hers was trembling freely. "I'll wait here until they return, dearest," he whispered. To the servants he said out loud, "Don't hang about, this is urgent!"

Bolli and Lambi, still blinking back their sleep, set off at once, while everyone else went back to bed.

Later on, we all got up and went about our business; and by mid-morning the two servants were back.

"Well?" demanded Uncle Egil before they had even caught their breath.

"There's five of them, Master – just a few miles down the road! They were going to let us ride past without so much as a greeting, let alone a scratch or bruise; but when we challenged them, they admitted immediately that they were waiting there for you. They thought you weren't home yet, but would be taking that road on your way back."

"Were they armed?"

"With a sword and an axe each, Master."

Uncle Egil let out a deep groan. "Didn't they know about the wedding? How can they . . ."

"They hadn't heard anything about it, Master. They were led by Grim Helgisson himself, but he hadn't been home yet, or seen his son. He said he only knew that you'd committed an outrage, and that because of it you had to die."

"Thank you," said Uncle Egil quietly. "Go and rest before you start work in the fields – you've done well. But first unsaddle my horses – I shan't need them today after all. And . . . send Kjartan to me here."

Through the open door, the day hung in a fine, grey summer mist over the fields.

"You wanted me, Master?"

It was Kjartan, slinking in as quiet as a mouse. How often did he pass through rooms and corners, unseen and unheard?

Uncle Egil swung round, jumping at the sudden voice.

"Ah, boy. Tell me: *how did you know?*"

"About Mistress Ingrid's dream, Master?"

"Yes."

Kjartan shrugged. "I just knew it."

"Come here and look me in the eye. Have you got the second sight?"

He shrugged again.

"How else could you have known it so exactly?" pondered Uncle Egil. He grabbed Kjartan by the ears, jerking up his face in its wild frame of black hair for closer examination. "You're not in league with this Grim and his band, are you? Eh? Tell me!"

"Of course not, Master."

"You're a queer fish," butted in Aunt Thorhalla. "You're as deep as murky waters. I wonder what else you know that's none of your business?"

"Oh, I know lots of things, Mistress." His voice was softly enticing, hinting of secrets. I felt him willing me to look at him. I tried my hardest to ignore it, but at last could hold out no longer. In the brief instant that he caught my eye, he mouthed the word "Ruadh" at me so clearly that he might have spoken it out loud.

"Well, whether it's the second sight or something more simple," said my aunt wearily, "you've served us well today. You've saved your master's life! Keep on like this, and you may grow up to earn your freedom after all. Now – go."

He went as he was told, piercing the back of my head again with his gaze.

50

CHAPTER 6

The Wedding

Some days later Uncle Snorri sent messengers to say that he and Grim had now had words together and that Uncle Egil had no more to fear. So it was arranged that the wedding feast was to be held at our own farm.

There was little time and a great deal to do: we forgot our worries in a whirl of scrubbing, cleaning and cooking. All the wooden carvings on the panelling and the doorposts had to be carefully polished; and the cushions and draperies beaten and put outside to air. Huge, fragrant bunches and wreaths of flowers were hung from every beam, and the floor strewn with a thick layer of new yellow rushes.

Uncle Snorri rode over with his party the day before the first guests were due to arrive. Gudrun's cheeks glowed with rosy contentment and she had combed her yellow hair until it gleamed.

"Come outside and talk, Ingrid, while the time's still our own," she said.

We wandered down to the river and settled ourselves in the long grass. She began to pick the tiny white blossoms that grew like stars among the blades.

"Don't you think they're pretty?" she said. "I'll wear some tomorrow with my wedding dress. What are you going to wear for the feast, Ingrid?"

"Oh, a dress that was my mother's best one, and her gold bracelet and finest brooches too. I'm not really supposed to touch them until I come of age. But Aunt Thorhalla said I could have them out specially in honour of your wedding."

Gudrun's cheeks flushed even pinker; she clasped her hands round her knees and gazed dreamily into the brown, bubbly water.

"*My* wedding!" she breathed. "At last it's really happening! I've waited so long, but now I've found Mord I know I shall be happy."

A huge bee droned lazily through the stalks; the wind had dropped completely, and for a few moments on that balmy afternoon it was as if life consisted of nothing but honey and weddings. We took off our shoes and stockings, and dangled our feet in the bitterly cold river, each lost in our own thoughts. Then, all at once, Gudrun said, "I'm glad you'll be wearing your best things, Ingrid. Mord's father will be interested to see them."

I sat up quickly.

"Mord's father –?"

"Yes, Grim. You've met him already, haven't you?"

"*Met* him?! Gudrun, I'm sure I shouldn't really mention it the day before he becomes your father-in-law, but did you know he was going to *kill* Uncle Egil?"

"Oh that," she gurgled soothingly. "Of course I knew. Mord's told me all about it. But it's over now that our families are to be joined. I believe Grim's going to let Uncle Egil pay a fine instead." I winced at her insensitivity. "Besides," she went on, "Mord tells me that Grim's got another reason for goodwill towards your family."

"What's that?"

"You," she said simply.

"Me?"

She pulled her plump feet out of the stream and watched the little beads of water drying from them in the sunshine.

"Apparently you've made quite an impression on him. He admires your spirit, he told Mord. That's why he was so interested to hear about your being an heiress. He's got his eye on you, Ingrid, see if I'm wrong! In fact, it wouldn't surprise me if he has words about you with Uncle Egil, as soon as they've agreed this settlement. Especially with him already having weddings on his mind."

"What are you talking about?" I demanded. "If he's trying to matchmake for any of his other sons, then he'd better not look at me! I'm far too young even to dream of marrying! Fancy you suggesting it, Gudrun."

"Oh, you silly," she giggled, "you've got it completely wrong, just as I knew you would. Mord's only got sisters."

"Thank goodness for that," I said. "So what's all this about?"

"I told you, it's Grim himself who's interested, no-one else. He's a widower, you know – Mord's mother died when he was a baby. *Grim* wants to marry you."

I blinked at her. "But he's an old man!"

"Yes, but he's ever so rich," said Gudrun, as if he had commissioned her to conduct the wooing. "He used to go on Viking raids to England every year, you know, so he's got heaps of gold and silver. It's not such a bad idea, actually – I've got two friends who married men of Grim's age and they say their husbands are always either away on business or fast asleep: they're hardly any bother at all. And of course, he'll die long before you do, and then he'll leave you all his money as well as your own inheritance."

"I don't want any more money!" I cried. "I'm looking forward to having all my mother's jewellery, and to running my own farm, but that's quite enough for me. In fact, I'm not sure that I even want a husband at all."

She took my arm and came so close in her earnestness that I could smell her rich perfume.

"But Ingrid, listen. Grim's got a huge farm with a wonderful house, and Mord and I are to live there with him. So if you married him, we'd all be there together. Think what fun –"

"Oh, Gudrun, how *could* you?" I threw a handful of

54

grass into her face and left her sitting there in her little cocoon of happiness, with the excuse that I might be needed indoors.

Back across the meadow, two more horses were tethered in the yard. I recognised one of them as Grim's, and my stomach turned a quick somersault as I saw him.

He was standing in the doorway, a great, red-haired hulk, shaking Uncle Egil's hand vigorously in a brawny, crushing grip.

". . . I'm so glad, I really am pleased," Uncle Egil was saying, "that things are working out so well now. Yes, yes, I'm certain we can come to . . . er . . . a satisfactory settlement, Grim, now that our families are to be united. Look, here comes my foster daughter – you remember Ingrid, don't you?"

Grim turned to me at once with a smile as oddly placed as a haystack in a snowfield, "Hello there!"

I squeezed hurriedly past them through the door. Uncle Egil was about to call me back, but to my relief Aunt Thorhalla's voice cut across, "Ingrid, come in at once to help! You've been messing about outside for far too long."

She was standing by the fire-pit, giving orders to the servants and slaves. Some were putting up brightly coloured hangings, others were busy polishing silver plates and drinking horns. I almost fell over the provisions that were piled all around: carcasses of lamb for the spit and huge earthenware vats of wine, specially imported from the south. The air was rich with a hundred delicious smells: the juices of roasting meat, fresh summer hay on the floor, and the sickly burning sweetness of alcohol. No wonder they chattered and sang about their work; and my aunt bantered jokes with them all.

For once even Kjartan had cast away his sullenness. He strode past, humming a strange, foreign-sounding tune, his eyes bright with merriment.

"What's up with you, slave boy?" I said.

He laughed and muttered something unintelligible under his breath.

"What did you say?" I asked sharply, grabbing his shoulder; but he twisted free of me and went on into the store-room.

"Leave him, Ingrid!" scolded Aunt Thorhalla. "No wonder the boy's a nuisance to you if you treat him like that. I've no idea why you object to him – he's been a great help today, and so polite to our visitors."

I scorned to hear such praise of the wretch. Yet when the hall was thronged with guests and merrymaking the next day, I was reminded of it again.

Uncle Egil was going round with Uncle Snorri, slapping everyone on the back, shaking hands and wishing each one well, when all at once I saw Grim taking him aside for a quiet word.

I had been offering round the wine; but, mindful of what Gudrun had told me, I put the flask down and crept behind the pillar where they stood, to eavesdrop.

To my immense relief, I wasn't the subject of their talk at all.

"That slave boy," came Grim's rasping voice, "the

shaggy, dark one with the surly eye. Have you had him long?"

"Well, to tell the truth, friend," said Uncle Egil, ever anxious to keep things smooth between them, "we bought him a good few years ago as a small child. He was sold as a bargain, but I must say that he's extraordinarily strong."

"I've taken a fancy to him," said Grim shortly.

"You'd like to . . . buy him?" ventured Uncle Egil.

Grim guffawed. "Buy him? Come, come, Egil, we have a settlement still to be finalised. I've had mercy on your life, even though our peace has yet to be agreed by the Law Chiefs."

He drew his sword from its scabbard and ran three fingers of his left hand thoughtfully along the blade. There was only a stump where the fourth should have been.

Uncle Egil's eyes followed his hand as it moved, down and up and down.

"Throw the lad in!" cried Grim. "If he fetches and carries as well as he's done today, he'll be a fine part of the compensation price."

"Perhaps then I might withdraw one of the cows?" suggested my uncle. "The boy's strength will be a loss to us and we'll be hard put to replace him."

"What!" exclaimed Grim, "withdraw part of the payment that we've already almost exchanged? Do you want to be thought of as a miser, as well as a harbourer of wizards? No, throw him in, Egil. That's right, let's shake hands on it."

He wheeled round to wave a greeting at someone across the room. Then, in his hurry to grab a mug of ale from a passing tray, he almost stumbled over me – with an exclamation of delight. Before I could be cornered, I slipped away and dived, for safety's sake, under a table.

But who should I find already crouched down there, munching his way through a greasy hunk of chicken thigh? None other than Kjartan!

He put his finger to his lips as a sign to silence.

"You can stop looking so pleased with yourself," I hissed. "A deal's just been done. My foster father's giving you to Grim as part of their settlement. I shouldn't think your new master will let you get away with such liberties."

He squatted there, watching me in the semi-darkness under the table, a forest of feet and legs on every side.

"Are you telling the truth?"

"Of course I am," I said, "and I'm so glad to think we'll be getting rid of you, I could dance for a hundred days!"

"Ingrid," he said; and then quickly corrected himself in a way that he'd never done before, as if he could not risk giving offence. "*Mistress* Ingrid – if I'm to be taken away, you've got to help me. Now."

"How dare you make demands of me, you . . . you worm!" I exploded. I had just made up my mind to have him dragged out and beaten, when he stopped me with a word and a look so piteous as to wrench my heart in two.

"*Please* help!"

"What's this about?"

"It's not for me," said Kjartan, "it's for . . . someone else. An old friend."

My breath suddenly felt tight and choked. "Ruadh?"

He nodded.

"But . . . do you think he's really still alive?"

"I know he is," said Kjartan quietly, with absolute certainty. His eyes glinted like coals in the gloom. I remembered the ease with which he had interpreted my dream.

"*Have* you got the second sight?"

He tossed his mane of hair and laughed. "Don't be stupid! No, I've told you, I *know* lots of things."

"How?"

"I've been out," he said, "lots of times, when the household's all been sleeping. I *saw* the ambush on the road that time, on my way . . . to meet him."

"To meet Ruadh?"

He nodded again.

I wanted to shake him. "Kjartan, tell me where he is."

"He's living on the edge of the Smoky Mountains," he said, "down south by Trout Lake. He's all right at the moment – I've caught him birds and fish to eat, and taken him cheese and bread, and there's lots of wild herbs to pick. But I don't know what'll happen when winter comes. Unless . . ."

"Well?"

"Unless you help him to escape."

All around us feet shuffled, crumbs and bones tumbled to the floor, and voices rose with the heady merriment of wine. No-one would take any notice of us now.

"I'd like to . . ." I said uncertainly.

"Then you can help me at the same time," he said

eagerly. "I'm going too. It's been bad enough with your family, but I'm certainly not going to sit back and let old red-beard Grim become my master!"

"What a cheek! I'm not going to help *you*!"

"Look, Mistress Ingrid," said Kjartan, "there's two things to get into that pretty head of yours. Firstly, I've told you a hundred times, I shouldn't be a slave. Secondly, I know too many things for you to dare refuse me now."

"Such as?"

"Such as that you didn't catch up with Ruadh that night when you rode after him. I know. But you found – the Sorcerer."

"How do you know that?"

"And you didn't tell anyone about it, although if you had done, he might well have been caught by now. So you've got a dark secret, haven't you, clever Mistress Ingrid? You know how high feelings are running against anyone who shelters the Sorcerer in any way. Well, I know your secret, and I also want your help. I'm good at keeping things quiet – but only if it suits me to."

I felt trapped, as the sea-birds must feel when a man stands over them with a net in his hand.

Gudrun's plump ankles walked past, and her bubbling laughter floated down like a taunt.

"All right then, slave boy," I sighed. "You'd better lead the way."

CHAPTER 7

Words in the Wilderness

We could not risk being seen leaving together, so I told Kjartan to set out first on foot, and that I would bring ponies and catch up with him further along the road. He slunk across the floor to the end of the table and disappeared, a thin dark shadow, out through the back.

Uncle Snorri had splashed out on a poet to entertain the guests, newly come from the court of the Norwegian king. Now the drinking horns were put aside and everyone settled comfortably to hear him, clapping and fooling about, laughing tipsily at his jokes and rhymes.

It was a good time to make an escape. I fetched a cloak and changed from my best dress into something more suitable for a journey on horseback; then I slipped out and made my way to the stables.

The yard was quite deserted. I saddled Ice Star and led her out, and for Kjartan chose her neighbour Storm Cloud, a pony as grey as his name.

We cantered out of the farm, up the grassy slope and onto the rough track that led south into the Smoky Mountains. It was the same road I had taken in pursuit of Ruadh on that fateful day at the start of spring.

The air was very still. The wind had dropped, and there was no sound but for the ponies' feet clop-clopping over the track, and merrymaking drifting distantly from our farm. The midday sun beat down, and for a short time I fell to day-dreaming.

All at once, there was Kjartan, blocking the road ahead, arms akimbo, grinning like a fox. He did not move until we were almost upon him; then suddenly he reached out to grab Storm Cloud's rein from my hand.

"What's this you've brought me?" he cried, looking with dismay at the pony's aged eyes. He swung easily into the saddle. "Well, Mistress Ingrid, even though you've insulted me with the most decrepit horse in the valley, I suppose you'd still like me to lead the way?"

He set off at a gallop. Ice Star would have followed suit, but I deliberately reined her in.

"Not so fast," I called, "you'll get the horses tired too quickly!"

His only answer was to urge Storm Cloud even faster

along the track.

Soon he was lost ahead, behind hillocks and boulders. I followed on Ice Star at an easy pace, and caught up with him at last when the sun had moved an hour across the sky.

He had stopped by a river bank, where the pastures started to thin into a rocky wasteland, and the water rushed over shingle in a roaring brown flood. Storm Cloud stood heaving and glistening with sweat, drinking great gasping draughts of water from the river. Beside him, Kjartan lay calmly stretched out full-length in the long grass, with a large rag thrown across his face to shade it from the glaring sun.

I dismounted and sent Ice Star down to drink.

"You're worn out already, and so is your horse. You're an idiot to rush like that."

"You should know," said Kjartan, without even bothering to sit up, "that a slave has no time to waste. That's what you've told me often enough, young Mistress Ingrid. Why are you so angry now, if I do things as I've been taught?" His voice came out muffled through the rag.

It deserved no answer. I walked upstream of the ponies and drank from cupped hands. "Come on then, if time's so short."

The grasslands were thinning out rapidly now, and fairly soon we reached their end. A vast expanse of grey, stony desert stretched ahead.

"This is where I usually see him," said Kjartan, drawing Storm Cloud to a halt. "When he's well enough, he walks to meet me here."

I gazed at the bleak, pock-marked carpet of rocks and ancient lava flows. After a mile or so it rose into smooth, ochre-coloured mountains, looming hard and barren like a giant's fortress against the sky-line. Their upper reaches were encrusted with crystals, and white, silent columns of smoke rose from secret springs and blow-holes in their midst.

"Which way?" I dared not look behind, in case I lost the courage to go on.

"Just follow me."

We began to ride carefully across the boulders, over dried-up water gullies and sudden gaping cracks in the ground. In front, the glistening hills grew steadily closer, until I saw that the track led into a sheer-sided valley between their slopes.

The silence became stronger as we penetrated the wilderness. It seemed to whistle in the ears, to cling at us and our surroundings, heavy as a formless layer of dust.

We were quite alone. Not even a single bird hung above us in the sky. There were only dry stones, cracked and crumbling to the jagged line of mountains on the horizon. Occasionally we passed startling clumps of tiny purple flowers, clinging to the earth in terror of the wind, and scores of brown, leggy spiders scurrying across the desert on secret business of their own.

"Kjartan," I said, longing for the sound of voices.

His back stiffened, but he did not turn.

"Kjartan, why are you helping Ruadh?" My words seemed to lose themselves in the emptiness.

He shrugged and rode unflinchingly on.

I gave up for a while; but as I gazed around, the Sorcerer's face seemed to lurk, sinister and forlorn, in every rock. I had to talk, just to shut out the singing loneliness.

"Please answer me!"

This time he waited for me to catch him up, so that now we rode side by side.

He said shortly, "No-one else cares about him. Like no-one cares about me."

"That's a soft answer, coming from you."

"I like him," he went on, "because he talks to me *properly* – like no-one ever has done before. He doesn't look down on me, or try to make me feel I'm the lowest thing in the world. He's the only friend I've ever had. That's why I've got to help him."

He broke off in abrupt embarrassment as we entered the pass between the Smoky Mountains. Empty space gave way to tight, high walls of sand, and the thick smell of distant hissing steam.

Presently he spoke up again, as if he had been continuing the conversation in his own mind.

"So he's the only one that I shan't do any harm to – when my time comes at last!"

I jumped. "What do you mean?"

He sat up, tall and straight in the saddle, and glanced at me for a moment, coldly, threateningly blank. I could see his muscles tauten and his voice came out clipped and fierce. "I mean – when I'm a free man, Ingrid – taking revenge for all the years they've kept me in slavery! I'm going to take the last drop that's due from every single person that's ever made me suffer!"

The words echoed back and forth, back and forth between the steep slopes.

"Where are you taking me to?" It was an effort not to let my voice break into a scream. I studied him furtively, to see if he was carrying any weapon: a small, all-purpose knife swung innocently from his belt.

"Ruadh can't possibly be living in a wilderness like this!" I said. "I'm going back."

But behind us, beyond the narrow pass, all I could see was desert, stretching flat and monotonous, pitted with pot-holes. The farmlands had shrunk to a fuzzy green streak on the furthest edge of the horizon.

"As for *you*, heiress," he said, ignoring my protests, "*perhaps* if you help enough, *perhaps* I might just let you escape with your life."

I shivered. Would anyone ever find me, I wondered, if he chose to kill me here?

"I can't do it all on my own," Kjartan went on. "Your people will be after me, if they find I've got away. Besides, I've got no money. I haven't any friends either, apart from Ruadh. Nothing or no-one that's any use. But you have."

He said no more for a while. I began to think longingly of the warm, merry feast we had left behind. I found the trick of closing my eyes and wishing myself back there until at last it almost seemed true . . .

"Watch where you're going!" he said sharply.

I sighed myself awake. "What are you going to do?"

"It's what *you* must do, heiress," he said. "Firstly, you must find a ship that will take us both away to Ireland.

66

Ruadh longs to go home – and he wants me to go with him. I may as well – at least I'll have my freedom, and there's nothing to keep me here. It won't be easy to find a crew that's willing to take a runaway slave and a foreign outlaw on board . . . but you're rich, Ingrid, you can bribe anyone with all the gold you've got!

"The other thing is this. You see, Ruadh's really ill, and he's old. All the tramping around he's done has worn him out. I'm sure he couldn't walk all the way to the coast now. So after you've fixed up the ship, you're to come here with horses for us both, Ingrid; you're to bring them here and then help us to escape."

"All that! But how do you expect me to . . .?"

In angry panic I again forgot to watch where I was going. My pony stumbled after his round a sharp bend; then I looked up to see we were emerging from the end of our mountain passage.

There before us lay a lush stretch of grassland, waving in a soft breeze, running down to a blue, shimmering lake. Perched incongruously in the middle of this pasture was a small hut.

CHAPTER 8

Herbs of Healing

Across the lush expanse of waving grasses, by the banks of the deep blue lake from whose waters rose strange mounds and turrets of grey volcanic mud, there was Ruadh.

We rode forwards as fast as we could, sending up startled birds and clouds of tiny transparent midges as we went.

The hut was round, made of mud roughly packed and smoothed together, filled out and strengthened in places with large stones. Ruadh was kneeling on the ground before it with his back to us, unaware of our approach. While we were still a short distance from him, Kjartan reined in and quietly dismounted, signalling to me to do the same.

In the still afternoon, we could hear the old man muttering, foreign phrases tumbling out from under his breath, in a musical, mesmerising rhythm.

"What's he doing?"

The thin, bent figure swayed backwards and forwards, backwards and forwards with the words. He stretched out his arms, one on either side, like a bird spreading its wings, and prostrated himself on the ground in a gesture of utter anguish. "Is it sorcery?" I asked, afraid.

Kjartan shook his head. "Sshh, wait until he's finished. It's only his way of calling on his God."

At length, the Irishman completed his ritual. He stood up slowly without turning, and would have gone straight into his little hut, but at that moment Kjartan called out, "Ruadh!"

He spun round at once, staring at us both for a long moment. Then the tension melted from his face and it creased into a smile.

"Why, Kjartan – a thousand welcomes! And you've brought the girl, the little lady who I'm sure tried her hardest to be kind. You're welcome too, my dear; but call me old, call me forgetful, upon my life, I can't recall your name."

"She's Ingrid," said Kjartan, so casually that I might have been *his* slave. "I've brought her to help. How are you, friend?"

"As well as I have a right to be," said Ruadh; but his warm eyes were dulled, and his words were broken by a small, dry cough. "Come Kjartan, come Ingrid, sit and rest with me for a while."

He took us into the little hut. It contained nothing except a raised mud bench, a few small pots and bowls, and a much-worn parchment book. Inside, it was dark, cool and tranquil.

"You must both be thirsty and weary." He fussed around, cushioning the bench with dried grass, and bidding us sit down. "Wait a moment, I'll fetch some water that'll taste as sweet to you as the dew!"

He took up two wooden bowls and shuffled out, down to a nearby stream that flowed into the lake. He was gone for no more than five minutes; yet he returned quite out of breath, and the bowls shook in his hand, sending a fine shower of silvery droplets to the ground.

"Drink!" he commanded merrily. He sat down between us on the bench, panting softly yet still beaming.

"I'm sorry," said Kjartan, "*I* should have fetched it. Has the pain been bad?"

"Why, Kjartan, I should be all right in a little while," replied Ruadh. But then such a fit of coughing seized hold of him that he could not speak for a full minute until it passed. "Only, you see, it's too far for me to walk now to the places where the herbs grow; and so the sickness creeps up on me again. But I mustn't complain. I'm alive, and you have come to me, so everything is good."

Kjartan jumped up at once. I couldn't believe how willing he'd suddenly become.

70

"Let me go for you! I'll get whatever you need! Is it angelica that you want?"

"Yes, Kjartan, that more than anything. You remember, I showed you once where it grows, where the stream bends and twists half-way up the hill? And see if you can't find a sprig or two of purple thyme; and also some hawksweed and dandelion, and some blue speedwell if you pass some on your way."

I thought I ought to go with him, but Ruadh cried, "Stay and talk with me, little lady. I need company as much as medicines."

Kjartan hurried out, leaving the two of us alone. For a while Ruadh sat serene and still without speaking; then he turned with a fatherly smile to pat my hand.

"Let's go outside," he said. "Summer will be over before you blink. We should enjoy the sunshine while we can."

So we went outside and sat in the pungent, tickly grass. Despite the niggling cough and the heavy rings under his eyes, he looked completely at peace.

"Ruadh," I said at last, not sure how to begin, "I'm truly sorry we sent you away. We . . . I didn't want to."

"No," was all he said. It was like a sigh of wind, hovering in the air and dancing off across the meadow.

"We risked our lives," I tried to explain. "They found out later – and almost killed Uncle Egil because of it. And . . ."

"And you met the villain they were after," said Ruadh unexpectedly. "You came upon the Sorcerer, the one they mistook me for. And you were afraid?"

I nodded, soothed to share the bitter secret with him.

"Fear passes," he said, "just like sorrow. I can tell you, there's been days and nights when *I* feared to the bottom of my soul: I've known weeks and months when I slept and woke in an everlasting pit of despair. Yet here I am today, safe, and basking in the sunshine."

He put a thin hand on my shoulder and pointed out across the view. "See how the sun shimmers and glimmers on the blue, sparkling water? See how it glitters in the distance there on the brown, shining mountains? With such a feast for the eyes, how can we possibly feel any sorrow?"

"What happened to you?" I asked.

"Now, you may be surprised to hear this," he said dreamily, "but years ago in Ireland, Ingrid, I was a very great man – a king! In those days I lived in a fine castle. I had a host of servants to fulfil my every wish. I feasted each day on wild boar, venison and tender ducklings, all richly roasted and served on shining silver dishes. I had poets to thrill me and harpists to play to me; I slept at night in the softest of goose-feather beds."

I closed my eyes and a picture of his lost kingdom grew richly in my mind.

"Then I got married, to a lady who was the kindest and best and cleverest in all the world, and as beautiful as a rose, to crown it all. There was never such a happy king and queen as we were! We'd only been married a year when she bore me a son. But with that joyful moment came the first darkness, for on the day that she gave birth to him, she died."

He paused and shook his head.

"Nevertheless, our son became a strong, handsome boy. To see him grow each day was as good as to see the sun rise! But four years later, almost to the very day, the second darkness began.

"That was when the Vikings started to come raiding on our coasts. *Your* race of people, Ingrid, though I hate to say it. They brought their swords and axes, and they went berserk – raging through our land, chopping off heads, arms and legs, up and down the farms and villages; looting our jewels, drinking our wine, attacking our women, taking what they fancied and whom they pleased, all the way to my very own castle door. And would you believe it, though I mustered men and drew up battle-lines, they broke through my defences; and though I swear I gave them every piece of gold I had, still it was not enough. Because, to top it all, in the end they took away my son."

I stole a look at his face. There were tears welling up in his eyes. He closed them briefly and let out an anguished sigh.

"I'm sorry," I murmured; and wondered whether any of my own relations might have sailed on that raid.

"They left me my castle, but it seemed empty as the wilderness. They left me my fine robes, but what was the use of them now? No-one could offer me any comfort except the priests; so in the end, like them, I gave away the few things I still had left, and took to wandering, as a beggar, up and down the land.

"It's a hard way to live and a sad way, but the glory of it

is that it gives you time to think. And as the years went by, I thought more and more about my son, wondering whether he was still alive and, if so, where he could possibly be.

"So I built myself a little boat, and set sail towards the northlands, on the trail of the Viking raiders. The wind blew me north and it also blew me westward. By the grace of God my little boat kept me safe and dry, until I reached this cold, wild country of yours."

His voice trailed away dreamily. For a few minutes he said no more. I waited. Gradually his face seemed to soften. Then he murmured, "However, I must end by telling you this, Ingrid: I am no longer in darkness now, for truly the sun has come to shine on me again."

Footfalls sounded in the grass behind. Turning, we saw Kjartan coming back, stumbling in his hurry to reach us with his load. In each hand he carried thick bundles of greenery, stringy roots and bright flower-heads, with more leaves and stems sticking out from where he had stuffed them in his shirt.

"I've brought as much as I could find," he said, throwing himself on the ground before our feet. He pulled out the plants one after another, a tangled mass of green, yellow and blue.

Ruadh crouched over them in delight. "Here's enough thyme to help me sleep for many nights. And all this fragrant angelica, to ease my tired limbs! You're a wonderful friend, Kjartan!"

"Shall we cook some for you now?" said Kjartan, flushing eagerly at such praise. "Shall we make a fire?"

Ruadh's reply was engulfed in another fit of coughing. Kjartan jumped up and beckoned me to follow him to a slope behind the hut, where windswept lumps of dwarf birch trees grew. Together we gathered armfuls of brittle twigs, and carried them back.

We kindled them in the tiny fire-pit in the middle of the hut, while Ruadh shuffled in with an iron cauldron of water to set on the flames. As it came to the boil, he began to pluck leaves from the herbs and to drop them into the bubbling brew. Soon a fresh, earthy-scented steam warmed the hut.

Kjartan fetched a bowl and helped Ruadh, still coughing and wheezing, to sit down. He scooped up some of the potion and put it gently into the old man's hands.

"Surely this will make you better?"

Ruadh was sitting directly in the shaft of light that shone through the door. As we watched him drink, the colour gradually came seeping back into his face.

"Ah, this is sweeter than honey to my poor, aching chest."

When he had finished, we all went to sit outside again, while he prepared the remaining herbs for hanging up to dry.

"Ingrid's promised to help," said Kjartan.

Ruadh looked at me quizzically.

"She has money and influence," explained Kjartan, as if everything had already been arranged. "She's going to fix up a passage to Ireland."

"If only you could, little lady!" sighed Ruadh. "Oh, to

be in my own gentle country again, with the green hills rolling away and beyond to Heaven!"

He went on sorting the herbs, while Kjartan dozed in the sun. I gazed past the lake to the hostile, smoking mountains that we must pass again on our journey home, trying to fathom some way of carrying out this task.

"Now, here's an odd thing," said Ruadh suddenly. "Look, I've found a strip of leather entangled among the stems. That will do just nicely to bind them up for hanging. I wonder where it could have come from?" He held it up to show us. "Anyway, I think I'll cut it into pieces, then I can bind each herb separately. Now, what have I done with my knife? How forgetful I seem to become! Can you see it anywhere?"

I looked around and spotted the knife in its sheath, lying on the ground at Kjartan's feet. I picked it up. At the same time, Kjartan's hand flew in consternation to his neck: before I could pass the knife to Ruadh, the boy had sprung at me and wrested it from my hand, leaping on in a single movement to the spot where Ruadh crouched.

"No, Ruadh – no, friend, leave it!" he begged. "Please don't cut it! It's mine! It must have got caught up when I was bringing you the herbs – I had no idea! Give it back to me – *please*."

"Well, well, Kjartan, whatever is the matter?" asked Ruadh, kind and good-natured as ever. "I had no wish to take or break something that was yours, if only I'd known. Have it back, of course. I'll tie the herbs with plaited grass stalks, and no matter. Here you are – but at least tell us what it is."

He pulled it free from the mass of plants and handed it back: a long, very grimy and tattered leather thong. It must have snapped and broken from excessive use and age. Another fragment of leather was suspended from it, roughly shaped into a tiny pouch.

It was this that Kjartan's jealous fingers examined most carefully, feeling it all over as if something precious were contained inside.

Then he knotted the break together and tested the whole length to make sure there was no danger of its giving way again.

"It's mine!" he repeated, putting it over his head to hang inside his shirt. "I've worn it ever since the first day I can remember. It's all I've got in the world!"

Ruadh shot him a long, searching look. But he said nothing, and went quietly back to sorting his herbs.

CHAPTER 9

Secrets and Silence

We stayed with Ruadh for another couple of hours, listening to the memories and longings that he spun out for us like a spider at its gossamer. At last, much comforted by the medicines, he said he was ready to settle down to sleep.

We said farewell, collected the horses and started back through the mountains. It was around midnight: the sun had disappeared and shadows swallowed our surroundings, so that the stillness of the desert was more intense than ever. Kjartan was subdued. He let me ride in front and was even quite civil when I stopped once to ask his guidance over the rough ground. So I thought I would try to make peace.

"I'm glad you took me to see him," I said.

But he only replied in the old, sarcastic vein: "Oh, it's nothing to you, heiress, whether he lives or dies. You'll only help him if it suits you."

Then he would say no more, but rode on in silence, gazing steadfastly straight ahead. Once he clutched hold of the leather thong around his neck as if it might hold the key to some secret; but when he saw me watching him, he let go of it at once.

Where the desert petered out to the first stretches of green farmland, we stopped. The sky was already streaked with dawn.

"You'll get a whipping when they find you again," I said, trying not to sound too unkind about it. "Would you rather ride ahead of me and get it over with, or behind to put it off as long as possible?"

"You don't mince your words, Ingrid, do you?" he said. "I can't imagine you wasting any tears over my punishment. Do you think I'm afraid to take it? I'm certainly not going to dawdle back behind *you*!"

With that he was off again, as fast as on the outward journey, until he was only a small, dark streak disappearing into the winding valley.

I took Ice Star at a comfortable trot, enjoying the freshness of the morning and letting her stop when she wanted, to drink from the river or to eat the lush midsummer grass. I was hoping that, after a day and a night of revelling, the hundred guests at home would be too drunk to notice or care about my absence.

But as I rounded a bend that brought our farm into distant view, three squat figures appeared in the road before me.

They approached at a snail's pace, all talking together without pause, stopping often to wave their hands about or for one to shake a finger in the others' faces.

It was the old crones, Groa, Helga and Vigdis.

"Well, sisters!" exclaimed Groa as we met, "who is this? It's a young girl, hot as a mud-pool, and her face all red and desperate as if she has something to hide."

It was hopeless to try to evade them – not these three whose food and life-blood was scandal. Oh, what twist of fate had brought them into my path?

"Why, it's Ingrid – Egil and Thorhalla's foster daughter!" laughed Vigdis.

"The wonder of it is," said Helga, "what's she doing here when she should be at home helping with her cousin's wedding? And why does she look so flushed with guilt, and not the least bit pleased to see us?"

"That's true," agreed Vigdis, nodding her head so vigorously that it looked almost ready to fall off. "Aren't we her friends? Didn't we take bread with her and her foster mother, less than a month ago?"

I felt on public trial, sitting there above them on my pony; so I clambered down and tried to think of something redeeming to say.

"That's right, Ingrid," said Groa approvingly, "I was wondering when you'd stop looking down on us as if you thought you were so superior." She shook a bony finger at me, the tatters of her sleeve blowing accusingly in the wind. "Now, tell us at once without further ado: are you or are you not a very wicked girl?"

I tried desperately to think of a convincing answer, but my mind was blank with tiredness, and my mouth had become too dry to speak.

Helga cried, "Don't leave it to her to make excuses, sister! Tell her what we already know. Tell her who we've already seen, not half an hour ago, riding for his life ahead of her back to the farm."

The three pairs of sunken eyes all peered at me, seeking some twitch, some involuntary gesture that would finally prove my guilt. There was no way out. I felt my lips trembling; and then, in a great, heaving flood-tide of relief, I gave way to the merciful oblivion of tears.

"It's no good crying, Ingrid," scolded Helga. "Unless of course, it's with shame. Have you ever heard of such a thing, sisters? A well-bred girl running off with a common, dirty slave!"

But, unexpectedly, Vigdis put her arm around my shoulders. At that moment her small movement of maternal comfort meant more to me than all the world. I sobbed and sobbed, shaking against her ancient breast while she held and patted me with clumsy tenderness.

"There, there, Ingrid," she said awkwardly. "Poor lamb, I know how it is when you need to cry so. Let's have pity on her, sisters – we can remember what it is to be young, can't we?"

"To be young, yes," said Helga severely. "But Odin All-Father knows that *we* were never so wild and wayward."

"But please listen!" I begged through my sobs. "It's not as you see it at all. I've done nothing wrong, I promise you. We've been to do someone a kindness."

"*We*, she says," nodded Groa grimly. "You see, sisters, she confesses at once that she was not alone. A kindness is always a good thing, Ingrid, but why such secrecy? Why choose to do it at this time, when you should be dancing at your cousin's wedding? Why, above all, should you creep off to do it with a *slave*?"

"Explain yourself, dear," urged Vigdis.

"I . . . I can't," I said. "Only *please* don't tell anyone that you've met me. I can't bear to think . . ."

"It's all very well you pleading like this," said Groa, "only you have to see it from our viewpoint too. It's not that we want to get you into trouble, is it, sisters?"

"Oh no, not trouble," they cried.

"Only we have a living to make and a life to lead and – look at us now . . ." She held open her arms so that I saw, beneath her cloak, a dress so old and mended that it was more patches than anything. "You see, we have nothing to buy us a crust but the stories that we find along the road."

A small ray of hope suggested itself.

"If you would promise – if you would swear by Thor not to speak a word of this to anyone – I would give you far more than a mere crust of bread."

"Now you're talking business, Ingrid," said Groa, her voice losing its stoniness at once. "You'll do well for yourself some day. What will you offer us?"

She held out her gnarled hand so greedily that I would have slapped it hard, had I dared. But what would have been the use? So instead I considered the jewellery that I still wore from the wedding.

There was my pendant, the present from Uncle Egil: no, I could not give that away. A brooch? But all I wore now were my everyday bronze ones, which would scarcely satisfy them at all. And then I remembered the heavy gold bracelet with its rich, twisting pattern that had been a gift to my poor dead mother when she was a bride.

With a hot pang of remorse, I pulled it off and handed it to Groa.

Their eyes grew big with delight – so big that I wondered if I had given them too much – and for the first time since our meeting they all broke into broad, toothless smiles.

"That is generous of you, Ingrid, very generous," said Groa. "You've bought our silence well. I swear – not just by Thor, but by all the gods in Asgard! – that we shan't breathe a word of what we have seen of you today."

"We too, by mighty Thor and the rest!" Helga and Vigdis exclaimed. "But come, Groa dear," they added hastily, "don't hog the gift, let us see it too."

They passed it around, caressing the twisted metal coils lovingly. "Sit down, Ingrid dear," continued Groa in her new tone. "You can't return to the wedding like this." She nudged me slyly. "People will wonder why you look so worn out and hungry."

We were standing in a sort of grassy hollow, and here they settled me down in their midst, transformed into a guest of honour. To my astonishment, from somewhere deep under the torn, dirty folds of their cloaks, the three beggar-women produced a mouth-watering picnic.

There was a whole juicy sheep's head, two large salted fish and a fat skin full of soft cheese. Finally, with a proud flourish, Helga produced a honeycomb, all dripping, sticky and sweet.

"Eat as much as you can, Ingrid," commanded Groa.

"But where . . . ?"

"Hush now," said Vigdis.

"Who will have some cheese?" offered Helga, squatting busily by the heap of food. "Ingrid? Or some fish?"

It was such a relief to eat and to be treated as a friend, that soon I began to relax. And to feel the stirrings of curiosity.

"Have you heard any new stories since you were at our house?" I asked.

"Now, what have we got, sisters?" mused Groa obligingly.

"You haven't forgotten already?" cried Helga. "We've been to the Fjords and seen the ships!"

At once I thought of Ruadh's escape, and my heart began to race. "Where were they going?" I tried hard not to betray how eager I was to know.

"They had been west and were going south," said Groa, wiping her mouth on the hem of her apron with a satisfied look.

"While we were there a fine ship came into land," explained Helga. "It had a fine man for its master too."

"Tell her everything," urged Vigdis. "She deserves more than just our silence for that fine piece of gold."

"You've heard of Eirik the Red, Ingrid," said Groa, picking up the bracelet again, as if to reassure herself of its worth. "The fellow with a quick temper and a violent sword, who was outlawed and sailed west-over-sea to find the new country of Green Land?"

I nodded.

"Well, the captain of this ship now in the Fjords sailed there with him, not five summers ago. Ulf Whitebeard, they call him. He left the Green Land settlement because he couldn't put up with Eirik's foul outbursts; and now he's sailing south to the islands of Britain with a great cargo of sheepskins."

"Is he going soon?" I asked.

They hummed and ha-ed, unable to agree.

"At any rate," said Helga, starting to wrap up the remains of our meal in clean cheesecloths, "this is for sure: he'll come back a rich man. For they say he'll be calling in at Ireland; and he's supposed to have more than enough in his cargo to earn him a fine pot of yellow Irish gold . . . Now, who'll finish this corner of honeycomb, eh? No-one? Then I'll take it for myself."

"Such greed, such bad manners, sister," scolded Groa, as they all stood up to go. They wrapped their tattered cloaks carefully about them, until there was no sign that the dusty folds concealed such a feast of pickings.

"Thank you again for your gift, Ingrid – you've done us a great honour!"

I watched them go. Then, my mind all a-whirl, I ran down to the banks of the river and drank long and deep to quench my thirst after the rich food. I washed my face in its cooling waters and tidied my hair as best I could.

Ice Star was grazingly happily near by. She came

quickly when I called her, and seemed glad as we cantered the last mile or so back to our farm.

There was no-one about outside. But the stables were still full with strangers' horses. I let Ice Star in and, as I rubbed her down, saw Storm Cloud peacefully asleep in the far corner. Then I hurried into the house.

It was not a moment too soon, for already the guests were finishing breakfast and getting ready to leave. Uncle Egil and Uncle Snorri sat side by side in the two high-seats, handing out gifts. Kjartan was busy clearing away drinking horns and dishes, as if he had never been absent at all.

I hovered in the doorway, shaking hands with people as they left.

"Ah, so you're Ingrid? So nice to meet you . . ."

"Your Aunt Thorhalla has told us all about you . . ."

"What a pity we didn't see more of you . . ."

Gudrun led out the wedding procession, hanging on Mord's arm, looking more pink and pleased than ever.

"Ingrid!" she exclaimed. "Where have you been? We've been looking all over for you! I've been wanting to invite you to come and stay with us soon." She must have noticed my hesitation because she added, "Grim will be away on business for two weeks before Corn Cutting: why not come then?"

So we agreed, and they rode off with all the wedding band on their trail.

I went indoors in a cloud of dread – to find my aunt and uncle so deep in conversation with Grim and Uncle Snorri that they took no notice of me at all.

"Oh yes, they're happy enough now," said Grim as I

slipped past him. His barbed voice sounded curiously blunted, as if it held back some secret grief. "But even I am afraid: the wizardry is growing stronger."

Uncle Egil gulped. "Grim, you've treated me generously! If I'd known it was him –"

"Nonsense," interrupted my aunt, "how could we possibly have known? But, friend Grim, be assured, we'll not rest now until the evil is chased out."

"You'll help us in any way you can, then, brother?" said Uncle Snorri anxiously. "My Gudrun is so happy now, but if anything should happen –"

"Don't fool yourself," said Grim gruffly, clapping his three-fingered hand upon Uncle Snorri's shoulder. "Things *are* happening. Another twenty sheep died in my valley before we left home for the wedding, and I don't know of a child that's been born alive and well for eighteen months at least. What future does that point to for the bridal pair, eh?"

He shook his great, shaggy head and his eyes clouded, more with sorrow than with anger. "If any man could destroy this cursed Sorcerer, I swear the whole of Iceland would sing his praises!"

Uncle Egil and Aunt Thorhalla nodded earnestly.

Grim stepped over the threshold, then hesitated, looking severely at each of them before finally resting his eyes on me.

"But if anyone's found helping or hiding the Sorcerer from this day on, I don't care who he is: in Thor's thunderous name, there will be no more mercy. Such a traitor should count himself as dead!"

CHAPTER 10

Sorcery

"I tell you, Ingrid, they're all talking about you!" cried Aunt
Thorhalla. She was sitting by the large upright loom at the
end of the living room. "They kept asking, 'Where was
Ingrid? We didn't see her at the wedding.' I made excuses
that you were helping out in the kitchen but I know very
well that you weren't. What are you hiding? You'd better
watch yourself, my girl: with all this sorcery about, who
knows what accusations will be made against you next!"

She stood up and started to thread long, pale warp

threads on the loom, shaking her head as she went on, "Oh, if only we'd known what evil we were getting mixed up with that night!"

I sat there staring at the floor, longing more than anything to explain myself.

"Aunt Thorhalla," I began at last, "if I could prove to you that it *wasn't* the Sorcerer that we –"

"How can you talk so recklessly?" She turned to me, her face sour with suspicion. "You creep around now and nurse such secrets, anyone would think you'd fallen under the evil one's spell!"

Uncle Egil wandered in, with a smile for me as always.

"Oh, leave the girl alone, Thorhalla. There's nothing wrong except that she's seen too much excitement. First a wizard comes to stay, next a gang of men try to take my life, and then a wedding. It's too much for one so young."

I held my tongue after that, brooding alone on Ruadh and the mammoth task I had been set. All the odds seemed stacked against it. I even sought out Kjartan, but now he avoided me with scrupulous politeness. I was crippled by a feeling of impotence, and so did nothing to try to organise Ruadh's escape.

Meanwhile, Gudrun sent a messenger to repeat her invitation. My aunt and uncle thought it would do me good to stay for a while in someone else's house. So, shortly before Corn Cutting, I rode over to their farm.

Gudrun ran out to meet me, carrying a basket full of flowers.

"Ingrid! I'm so glad you've come at last!"

She hugged me and drew me cheerfully indoors. But

there was something about her manner that did not seem quite right: her smile was a mask that disappeared as soon as she turned away.

"You've no idea what fun it is to be in charge of my own house! And now you can help me, Ingrid – there's so much to do!"

I laughed, because dear Gudrun had never been keen on work: it was a family joke that she herself usually shared. This time, however, she did not join in; well, she tried to, but her eyes stayed deadly serious.

"Where's Mord?" I asked.

"Out in the fields. Checking the sheep. He'll be back before dinner. He's looking forward to meeting you properly."

"And you're happy, Gudrun?" I asked anxiously.

"Oh yes." She didn't sound as if she meant it. "As happy as . . . as can be." And with that, she burst into tears.

"Whatever's wrong?" I asked, fearing that she'd found some fault with Mord.

"Oh . . . oh, poor innocent Ingrid, you're so cut off in your farm: Uncle Egil makes sure of keeping you tucked away from trouble!" Her breath came in long sobs and her soft, plump body shook most piteously. "But all around here . . ." She gave way again to tears.

"Tell me."

"Well then, here it is short and sharp," she said, drying her eyes and making a real effort to cheer up. "Firstly, every single sheep and cow we have is weak and sickly."

She blew her nose noisily on her apron.

"And secondly, I'm expecting a baby."

"Gudrun, that's wonderful, congratulations! When's it to be born?"

Instead of looking joyful, she only shook her head. "Listen, Ingrid, supposing I'm struck by this dreadful curse? Supposing our baby . . ."

I bit my lip, while thoughts chased their tails like dark, swirling fishes in my mind.

We passed the afternoon in uneasy amusement, with Gudrun showing me over the house and farm, until Mord came home for his dinner.

He was large, sandy-coloured and silent – not a bit like his father. There was not an inch of gruffness about him: indeed, he had a manner of unguarded softness towards his wife.

"Two more," he muttered, chewing on a hunk of mutton.

"Dead?" asked Gudrun, trembling.

Mord nodded. "Yes, beloved. Just outside the home-field. And another nine lambs sickening."

Gudrun had lost her appetite: she picked at her food and, despite her pregnancy, seemed only to grow thinner as time went by. I stayed with them for eleven days, and each evening the news was the same. Gudrun and Mord began to talk of leaving their farm – perhaps even of sailing abroad.

"We can't do anything before I've discussed it with my father," said Mord.

"He's due back tomorrow or the day after, isn't he?" said Gudrun. "Perhaps we can tell him then."

"I know what he'll say," said Mord shortly. "A man can't run away, Gudrun." He sighed. "I'll have to stay here and fight."

"But in fighting, you yourself might be killed!"

"Perhaps I must be, for the sake of our child," replied Mord solemnly, "and for the health of our homeland. My father won't rest until the place is rid of sorcery, and nor will I."

When he had gone out I said to Gudrun, "You know I don't want to meet Grim, and you've made me welcome for long enough. I think I should go home this morning."

"How I wish you didn't have to go, Ingrid! You help me forget my troubles. But I suppose you can't stay here for ever."

She said that it wasn't safe any more for a girl to travel on her own, and made me promise to ride with one of their servants. But his chatty, deferential company was irritating, when all I longed for was to be quiet and to think. So after we had crossed the first river, I bribed him with silver to leave me without telling Gudrun, and finished the journey alone.

It was a pleasant ride, up hills, down dales, through masses of flowers and lush grass all the way. The only discomfort was the wind, which on the tops was so strong as almost to blow me from the saddle.

Three times along the track, I passed the slowly rotting bodies of sheep that had dropped dead where they stood. There was something unnatural about the way they lay there; and why had no ravens come to pick them clean?

I got down and crouched to examine one more closely. Standing up again, from the corner of my eye I saw a thin, fleeting shadow that vanished in a flash behind the high brow of the next hill.

By the cold creeping of my flesh, I knew at once who it must be.

I jumped back onto Ice Star and dug my heels in to urge her on. There was scarcely any need: she surged forward as if a thunderbolt had touched her nerves. We raced to the top of the hill and started after the shadow, down the other side. But the whole place was empty and deserted.

I reined in and stopped to look around. There was nothing but a hundred long fallen boulders, grey and shining in the sun, ridge after ridge of rich, wet grass, and the last river before home.

The wind blew the hair into my eyes so that I could scarcely see; it stung through my thin summer cloak, and sent shivers of goose pimples all down my body.

"Let's go," I whispered to Ice Star.

Down the hillside to the river we galloped. There were no dead sheep in this valley, but nor was there any sign of life. Not a bird or even a spider: only the piercing wind.

A hundred paces along the rushing grey river was a shallow ford which joined the main track back to our farm. Ice Star splashed through and we turned thankfully along it. Almost at once, I became aware of something else – a presence – lurking behind.

Stop slowly, I thought to myself. Turn to see who it is without showing any fear. I could hear the water hurtling over rocks a short way off, and the gale groaning angrily down the valley. I stopped, I turned.

It was not the Sorcerer after all. It was a boy with dark, close-cropped hair. I blinked and stared at him. It was Kjartan.

"You!" I cried, unable to disguise the relief in my voice. "Where have you sprung from, slave boy? And what have you done to yourself? What's happened to your hair?"

He patted the neat, sparse locks self-consciously, his black eyes shining larger, wilder, now that you could see more of his face.

"It's my disguise," he said softly. "What's the matter, Ingrid? You look all white."

I swallowed. "Have you seen . . . anyone else on the road? Or on the hillside?"

He shook his head. Oh, if only he could have shared my fear! "You can guess where I've been," he said hurriedly, before I could get in with anything else.

"Ruadh?" I whispered.

"I've met him twice more at the edge of the wilderness. But yesterday he wasn't there, so I walked all the way out to the lake." No wonder he looked so travel-weary: it was a long way to go on foot. "He was on his bed, Ingrid – the sickness is worse. That's why I came straight on, looking for you. You've got to arrange things for him. At once!"

In my mind's eye, the shadow eddies of menace cleared. Now I could only think of Ruadh's gaunt, kindly face, bathed in pale sunlight. Supposing he should never see his home again – because of my doubts and delay!

"I've . . . heard news of a ship," I faltered, still trying to shake off the last dregs of fright.

For a second, our eyes met.

"I . . . I'll go to the Fjords . . . very soon," I said, "and arrange a passage."

"Soon!" he cried, "soon may be too late! Do they know

you're coming home today?"

I shook my head.

"Then go now, Ingrid – if you care about him at all!"

Far along the track, smoke from my own farm rose steadily, welcomingly into the clear air. I sat on Ice Star, watching it while Kjartan waited.

"All right," I said at length, and turned to face northwards – the road that led to the Fjords.

"You'll be ready to fetch him when I get back?" I said.

"You won't find me at your home, Ingrid," he said quickly. "I'm leaving now. That's why –" He patted his shorn hair ruefully. "They tell me Grim Helgisson's coming for me tomorrow – I had to get out before that."

"But Kjartan – a runaway slave! You know what'll happen when they catch you . . ."

He shrugged. "I'm heading straight back to Ruadh. He needs me. I hope you'll find me there. But . . . if they should get me first . . . you'll look after him, won't you, and see him safely on his way?"

I nodded, not knowing what to say.

"Well then, what are you waiting for, heiress? Why do you always waste precious time? There's no point being miserable about my fate: it's your family who have brought it on me, after all. Think of that when you're lying soft in your feather-bed in years to come!"

"It's not my . . ."

"Stop arguing, Mistress Ingrid, and get on with it!"

Before I had time to cry out against the insolence of his command, he had thumped Ice Star's flank so hard that she went galloping off along the road.

CHAPTER 11

Gold for a Sea Passage

The scent and sound of the sea filled the air while it was still some way off. Gulls came screeching and gliding on the wind and the black-capped terns came darting and diving after them. The taste of salt brushed my lips and drew me, with a deep, inexplicable yearning, on towards the waves.

At last, the track emerged at the top of some towering cliffs. I looked down, down to the dark water of the fjord. A small, turf-roofed house and outbuildings nestled under the shadow of the rocks; and near by a wooden ship rocked its great swan-breast gently in the water alongside the quay.

I rode carefully down the steep track, while the birds wheeled around my head. At the bottom I turned straight past the buildings and made my way to the ship.

There was nobody there at all.

Up and down, up and down, the huge hull shifted in the water, ropes creaking, grinning dragon-head straining out towards the open sea. I sat motionless on Ice Star, awe-struck by the vessel's size and power; and then all at once a girl's voice behind me said, "What's your business, stranger?"

I spun round. She was scarcely older than me, tall and thin, with a washed-out look: her hair and long eyelashes were fine and almost colourless.

"I'm looking for a man called Ulf Whitebeard," I said, dismounting and tethering Ice Star to an iron ring in the quay.

"He's my father," said the girl. "Why do you want him?"

"I've . . . I've a message for him," I said quickly.

"Who's it from, stranger?" Her questions came at me like little sword thrusts.

"Is your father sailing soon?" I said, ignoring this last one.

She blinked her pale lashes at me. "I *could* tell you where my father is," she said, "but I won't unless you say why you want him. I don't know yet whether to trust you."

"All right, listen," I said. "I've got a friend who's in

97

trouble. He's a good man but he's been made an outlaw –
by mistake. He needs a passage southwards – quickly. Do
you think your father would help?"

"He's with my brothers," she said. "They're making
barrels and oars for the voyage." Her eyes, pale grey like a
gull's wing, had grown wide with interest. "I don't know
what he'll think of your story. And he certainly won't
help you for nothing."

"I realise that."

"Wait here, then."

She ran into the yard and disappeared into one of the
outbuildings. Five minutes later she was back.

"Follow me."

In the gloom of a long low shed, six men were bent
over planks and hammers, sending hollow shuddering
bangs into the air. It smelt fresh and dry, of wood
shavings. They were all of them tall, thin fellows, with the
same bleached hair and skin as the girl. Five were clearly
brothers; but the sixth was twenty or thirty years their
senior. His lean face was creased with many lines,
particularly around the eyes, as if he were always
wrinkling them against the light; and his beard was as
white as driven snow.

"I am Ulf," he said. "What do you want with me, girl?"

I felt like a slave on show at market, the way they all
stared at me.

"I've got a friend who urgently needs a passage south
to Ireland." My voice rang out shrilly in the hollow room.

"What will you give us if we take him, girl?" said Ulf
Whitebeard, "– apart from yourself!" He had the same

98

blankness of manner as his daughter, who still hovered behind me in the doorway.

The five brothers laughed loudly.

"There's not much of herself to give!" cried one.

I felt hot with embarrassment. "I'll give you gold!" I shouted, to stop their jesting.

"Whose gold?" demanded old Whitebeard, throwing down a handful of nails and striding across to me. I shivered as he came closer, for he had an aura about him that made me think of glaciers and icebergs.

"It's mine, sir," I said, as boldly as I could. "My own gold."

"Show me some. Now."

I hesitated.

"Stupid girl, do you think I'd snatch it from you and give nothing in return? Give an old sea-dog more honour to his name than that!"

"Here's one thing. I've got more at home."

Reluctantly I unfastened my gold Thor's Hammer to show him. He took it from me and scrutinised it long and close, then handed it back.

"That's not bad. So, then, tell me: who's this friend?"

"Oh, a . . . poor man," I faltered. "He came here long ago from the south, and now he's homesick."

"He's an outlaw, Father," said the girl suddenly from behind.

"So!" cried Ulf. "What crime has he committed to be beyond the leeway of the law?"

"Nothing," I said. "It's all a terrible mistake."

"I've heard that sort of feeble excuse before. Where are you from, girl?"

99

"From Trout River Dale, sir."

Ulf Whitebeard stiffened at the name. "You're the second from those parts to come seeking help here this summer," he said. "The other was a fellow called Grim Helgisson. Do you know him?"

"Yes."

From behind me the girl whispered, "If you're trying to trick us, stranger, we'll soon find you out!"

"I wonder if you know what he was doing here?" His voice was sharp with suspicion.

"No, sir."

Ulf was not a man to waste words. "This Grim was looking for a sorcerer," he said bluntly. "Is that your friend?"

The girl gave a little gasp.

One of the brothers muttered, "She looks stupid enough to befriend a wizard!"

I felt incensed at that: it gave me new courage.

"Do you think," I cried, "that I'd have the cheek to ask a great adventurer like you to help a villain? Well, you've asked me straight, sir, and I'll tell you straight. He's not a sorcerer, this friend of mine. But he's a foreigner, like the real outlaw that they're looking for. And because of that, there's lots of ignorant idiots who'd probably accuse him of committing the same crimes. But I swear by Thor himself that my friend is a good and honest man. He's innocent! In his old country he suffered dreadfully from Viking raiders, through no fault of his own. He deserves help!"

"You've got a hot tongue in your head, girl," said Ulf

approvingly. "If you were a man I'd challenge you to fight for a favour – or maybe take you into my crew at once." He smiled icily. "Now, what's your name?"

I told him.

"Well then, Ingrid, perhaps I will help you. But I never make unconditional bargains. I'll be frank with you: I'm a man who longs to grow richer. That's why I'll agree to your scheme and willingly take your gold – when we've fixed upon a price. But there must be three conditions on it."

"What are they, sir?"

Behind me his daughter was muttering, "Oh, all for a bit more gold! What trouble are we letting ourselves in for now?"

Ulf Whitebeard sat down on a half-finished barrel and fixed his watery gaze unwaveringly upon my face.

"Firstly," he said, "I won't accept any stranger on my ship, however much he swears to be the one you name, unless you yourself bring him to me."

I thought of more absences from home, more questioning from Aunt Thorhalla, and at the end of it all, what would there be? Only Ruadh gone for ever and a web of accusations for myself.

But I had my honour. I bit my lip hard with the finality of it and said in as steady a voice as I could muster, "I'll bring him to you, Ulf Whitebeard."

"But that's not the end of it," he went on. "He can't come here openly if, as you say, men are mistaking him for an outlaw. You must arrange for a disguise."

"How should I disguise him, sir?"

101

Ulf shrugged impatiently. "Must everyone leave all the thinking to an old man? I have sons, let's hear what ideas they can suggest."

But they came up with nothing but crude jokes that I blushed to hear.

"Shame on you!" cried Ulf, but laughing heartily nevertheless. "I can tell we'll have to ask your little sister. Thurid, I can see you lurking there in the shadows. Come forward and let's hear what you have to say."

She went to him sulkily. "If I were doing what she's doing, I'd dress my friend as an old woman. And if anyone asked our business, I'd say that this was my Irish nanny who'd grown too old to work and was going home to die."

"Well spoken, Thurid," said her father, glancing in my direction to check that I did not flinch from the tasks that were set. "Perhaps you can also help with the final and most crucial condition, which is this: how shall we make Ingrid prove that the man she brings really isn't the dreaded Sorcerer? And what revenge shall we take, if she turns out to have deceived us after all?"

Thurid looked at me with such distaste that I could not doubt her total lack of trust.

"She should swear by Thor to test the man publicly," she said. "As soon as she brings him to us, she should offer herself up to be the next victim of his spells."

"Do you swear it, girl?" cried Ulf Whitebeard, nodding and holding out his own large iron Thor's Hammer that hung from his belt.

I so longed to get all this over with that I grabbed the

charm at once and swore as I was told.

"And for payment," said Ulf, getting up and going back to his carpentry, "I ask for no more nor less than ten ounces of gold."

"Ten ounces!" I exclaimed, suddenly realising I would have to smuggle out that vast sum from the inheritance that Aunt Thorhalla kept under lock and key until the distant day when I came of age.

"Not half an ounce less!" he barked at me; and then the sound of his hammering drowned any protests I might have made.

I followed Thurid out to where Ice Star was tethered by the towering ship. She offered no comfort.

"I've been having bad dreams lately," she said, "and *you* have been in them. No good will come of this, you can be sure."

With that she disappeared into the house, leaving me alone with my fear and a long lonely journey home.

CHAPTER 12

Viking Treasure

"Well, here's Ingrid at any rate," called Aunt Thorhalla as I rode into the yard. Uncle Egil came rushing out from the house and greeted me as if it were years rather than days since he last saw me.

"Ingrid, welcome back! Have you enjoyed your stay with your cousin? Let's have a look at how you are."

He regarded me with a great beam of affection.

"I'm fine," I said as brightly as I could. "How are things here?"

"Dreadful," said Aunt Thorhalla shortly. "The plague

has spread to our own sheep, and as if we didn't already have more than enough to worry about, now we've got to deal with a runaway slave."

"Who's gone?" I tried my best to sound innocent.

"Only Kjartan," said Uncle Egil, "and I've no doubt that *you'll* be glad to hear it. But what a time to go missing! We were just about to send him to Grim as the last part of our, er, settlement. Goodness knows what the old rogue will do now if I can't complete it. Where could the lad have got to? He must know that a runaway slave has no rights in the law. Thor forbid that he should be tangled up in all this evil . . ."

Threshing the corn and churning the milk into butter; watching the flocks, and seeing the dead lambs being taken away to be burnt; eating and drinking and discussing the news, which seemed all shadowed with creeping fear. Never had a day been so slow in passing! And so at last to bed.

As soon as the last breath in the house gave way to snoring, I was up.

No Kjartan to confront me this time, I thought, with an unexpected twinge of regret. There was a chillness in the night air, and I shivered.

Nothing disturbed the darkness of the hall, except for the soft rhythms of sleep and a comforting crackling from the embers of the fire . . . And the pad-pad of my bare feet, creeping like a thief's across the cold mud of the floor, over to the place where Aunt Thorhalla slept.

The dying fire gave out just enough light to see the wooden bed-closet with its carved panels, a mass of twisting tendrils and stems. I felt for the catch on the door. It swung open easily, with a small, groaning creak.

Aunt Thorhalla stirred and half opened her eyes. I froze, melting back into the shadows.

"Who is it? Egil?"

I did not dare even to breathe.

"Oh . . ." she muttered thickly, "it must . . . be . . . a dream . . ." And then she was snoring again.

I inched forward. Ah, there were her keys! – a great heavy bunch of them, carefully placed upon a shelf by her head. My hand closed over the cold metal, and I believe that the gods heard my prayer that they should not jangle as I brought them out.

Back across the hall, down to the platform at the end on which the storage chests all stood. The last coals shifted in the fire-pit and almost died.

I knew exactly where to find the coffer containing the small fortune that one day would be mine.

One day – yet there I was, stealing from it now, long before my due. What would happen if this latest crime should be added to the others that, so far, my uncle and aunt had scarcely even guessed at?

I held the keys carefully and tried one in the rusty lock. It clicked loudly in the stillness, but would not turn. I withdrew it, then waited a few moments, in case the noise had disturbed anyone. But the household slept on peacefully, as if they were under a spell.

The third key I tried was the right one: it turned stiffly, but at once.

I had never seen inside that chest before. I only knew

106

that, added to the farm I would one day own, it contained enough to make me a very rich woman indeed. But I had no inkling of exactly what form my fortune might take.

So when I threw back the lid and saw within such a great hoard of treasure as might be gathered from the ends of the world, I almost cried out loud with wonder.

I found myself looking into a bottomless pit of silver and gold. Ornaments, caskets, jewels, chains and precious ingots glinted up at me in the blackness, like miniature suns and moons.

I put my hand inside and my heart skipped a beat to feel the coldness of the metal, real as day, against my skin.

Viking treasure! Bought dearly from the ravaged coasts of Europe, paid for with blood and terror and, ultimately, my father's life. One day all of it, misgotten as it was, would legally be mine.

When it had been won with so much sorrow, why should I feel remorse at taking it before my time? Particularly if in doing so I could help someone who had lost his own treasures to such ruthless Viking greed?

Ten ounces of gold, Ulf Whitebeard had asked for. Well, I would certainly not pay him short. But how to choose? I closed my eyes, felt inside at random and pulled out a large golden chalice. It seemed heavy as rock as I weighed it in my hands: surely it would be enough? Placing it gently on the floor, I closed the lid and locked it, then crept back to replace the keys by the side of my sleeping aunt.

The gold glimmered with a dull, yellow lustre in the darkness. I picked it up and, wrapping a cloak about my shoulders, hid it carefully under the folds.

107

Out then into the cold night air with the first hints of sunrise already creeping over the hilltops to the east.

I would not take Ice Star out again after riding her so hard yesterday. Instead I chose Aunt Thorhalla's pony, a brown mare called Spinner, and led two others behind me, for Ruadh and Kjartan.

Dawn bled across the sky. The track grew more distinct and boulders emerged from the vague greyness: on either side green pastures were revealed, and the slowly moving forms of sheep.

Something else unfolded with the day: I was haunted, for the second time, by the certainty of a presence near by.

Somewhere – whether before me or behind there was no knowing – somebody else was travelling.

On the nearest slopes, a sheep bleated eerily, looming out of the twilight with its fleece dropping from its back in tatters.

I turned round. As far as the eye could see, there was nothing in any direction. Yet I knew, beyond the smallest grain of doubt, that somewhere that night the Sorcerer was on the road.

The three ponies went steadily onward. Once I actually fell asleep and only woke when they stopped, finding themselves in that strange place where the farmlands gave way to the desert. It was completely light now, but even so I wondered whether I would find my way over the treacherous chasms and rocks.

The animals snorted uneasily at the barren landscape and the unearthly smell that floated across from the steaming mountains. Perhaps they could also sense my uncertainty. I dozed again and let them pick their own way.

Then suddenly, coming towards me across the lava field, there was Kjartan!

I jerked awake, gladder than I should have been to see him, and urged the horses on.

He stood and waited, silhouetted against the sky.

"So you've come at last, heiress," he said accusingly as I reached him.

"Don't speak as if I've just been hanging around!" I retorted. "I've come as soon as I possibly could. I've fixed up Ruadh's sea passage, and I haven't slept for two nights – what more do you want?" Tears of weariness pricked at my eyelids. I blinked them furiously back before they could give him any satisfaction. "Now get up on one of the horses if you want it, and let's go!"

He did as I told him. But every few minutes he turned his cropped head to look at me over his shoulder. At last, in the middle of nowhere, he drew to a halt.

"What are you carrying under your cloak, Ingrid?"

"That's none of your business."

"I want to know what you're hiding!"

He came back and lunged across at me, trying to grab at the fat bundle of the chalice. But I was too quick: I kicked him hard, so that his horse reared up and would have sent him flying, only he clung on like a desert flower to the rocks.

He regained his balance with a laugh that rang into the wide emptiness. But he nursed his shin: I had made my point.

"It's gold," I said quietly, "to buy Ruadh's passage." He did not ask to look at it again.

The morning was already old when we rounded the blue lake and crossed the lush grassy slopes to where Ruadh had his camp. The old Irishman was squatting in front of his hut, carving rune-letters into a large, flat stone with his knife. He rose at our approach and came hobbling towards us, beaming with pleasure, despite the ever-troubling cough.

"No no, rest yourself," fussed Kjartan, jumping down and leading the old man gently by the arm back to his seat.

"Let me be, Kjartan," chuckled Ruadh. "Won't you allow me to bestow a thousand welcomes on my two most cherished friends? Here you are back already with dear Ingrid: who shall say that Ruadh isn't lucky! Come on now, come inside."

We went into his little hovel, where Kjartan had left him a fire burning. There was nowhere to sit down, for the mud bench was cluttered all over with a litter of wilting leaves and flowers.

"Brush yourself a little space to sit, if you will, Ingrid," said Ruadh. "You must excuse the untidiness, only Kjartan has been brewing me my herbs."

"You should have cleared up after yourself," I hissed at Kjartan as I found myself a seat.

"I've got more important things to do than keep a house tidy to please hoity-toity visitors," he returned. "If you're offended by the lack of polish, you'll have to see to

110

it yourself, because I'm going to fetch more firewood." He hurried angrily out of the door.

"Such harsh words between you!" exclaimed Ruadh sadly when Kjartan had gone. "Still, you're both so young. I dare say you'll mellow. Now, I hope you'll excuse me if I go outside again, Ingrid, where the light's brighter, so that I can finish my work."

He went out and I followed him. We sat side by side, leaning against the door frame. The sun weighed warm and comforting on my eyelids, as he bent patiently over his carving.

He did not talk much, but hummed softly, a tune as sweet as bird-song.

I glanced across to watch the spiky letters slowly taking form:

Ruadh lived here. He has . . .

But before he could carve any more, I had fallen fast asleep.

CHAPTER 13

Make Haste!

Late in the afternoon I opened my eyes to find myself lying inside the little hut, on a soft mattress of hay. Kjartan appeared in the doorway and began to reprimand me: "Get up, heiress: you'll have to shake off your rich, lazy ways! We've an escape to make and it all depends on you."

"By all that's good, leave her, Kjartan," protested Ruadh, shuffling in behind. "It's been a treat to watch her sleeping."

I sat up. "What time is it?"

"Late," said Kjartan. "Now hurry!"

I got up and ran down to the river to wash the drowsiness away, still smarting at the thought of Kjartan giving me orders.

Back in the hut, he and Ruadh were boiling trout in a pot over the fire. It was sparse food compared to what I was used to. Nevertheless, the sight and smell made me ache with hunger.

Ruadh served up the meal, keeping the smallest portion for himself.

"Let's make this a feast to good fortune," he said. "Eat and be thankful. And then, Ingrid, you must tell us everything without wasting words, for the hours are draining away."

Kjartan ate in silence, watching Ruadh anxiously. Once, when the old man looked away, Kjartan actually spooned some of his own fish onto Ruadh's plate. But Ruadh merely played with his food and seemed scarcely able to manage the small helping that he already had.

I told them about Ulf Whitebeard, his coming voyage to Ireland, our agreement and his bargaining, including the three conditions he had laid down. But I did not mention the price he was asking, for that was my business.

"It sounds a fair plan, heiress," said Kjartan grudgingly. "Where's Ruadh's disguise?"

In the rush of my departure, I had forgotten that completely.

"Fool! How are we to meet Ulf Whitebeard's conditions now?"

"Don't fret yourselves," said Ruadh gently. "Look here,

113

I have a large blanket. Surely with a little imagination we can fold and stitch it into a dress? So – I'm to end my days in Iceland as a woman!" He chuckled heartily, but gave way almost at once to a searing, wheezing cough. "Ah me, all this talking is too much, too mu-u-uch!"

If he was in pain, he would not admit it for the world. He took great delight in folding his blanket, then cutting it into shape. For a needle he picked out a large fish bone, filing it to a point with his knife and then threading it with unravelled yarn. His cloak and boots would have to suffice as they were.

"But what about your beard?" I cried suddenly, as I stitched away at the last hem. "You'll never pass as a woman with that."

He handed Kjartan his knife. "Cut it off, friend," he said firmly, "cut it close and smooth."

When the last grey wisps had fallen to the ground, he smiled ruefully. He looked raw and hollow-cheeked, yet somehow more imposing.

"Keep a strand of it each for memory's sake. You can throw the rest to the wind."

It was a slow journey through the mountains and wilderness into the farmlands. Ruadh sat huddled uncomfortably on his pony, shielding his face deeply under the hood of his cloak. We had to stop often, to relieve him from the constant jogging, to drink from a spring and, when we could persuade him, to eat. Not that there was much food to find, other than herbs and berries.

When darkness fell, we made camp in a grassy hollow

by the river and Kjartan stoned three plump brown birds, which we roasted over a makeshift fire. After that simple meal we all slept until the early dawn.

We were soon on our way again. We skirted my farm widely, adding another four or five miles to the journey. At last we joined the road. But scarcely had we started on the last stretch to the Fjords, when, with a sinking heart, I made out Groa, Vigdis and Helga hurrying along the road towards us.

"Those three!" I cried. "They always appear at the worst possible moment. The news of us will be all over Iceland in no time!"

"I cut my hair so that no-one would recognise me," said Kjartan quickly. "Let me do the talking. Hide yourselves well."

So Ruadh and I folded our cloaks and hoods more tightly around us. Then we rode steadily on to meet the aged trio.

"Greetings to you all," called Groa as they peered at us suspiciously. "The road this way leads nowhere but the sea, you know."

"Greetings," returned Kjartan, with such politeness that I hardly knew him. "It's the sea we're off to. We're looking for a ship that might take our old nanny home to Ireland. She's past working now, and it's not fair to let her waste away here amongst the wizardry and sickness."

"What a kind heart you have," approved Groa with a touch of envy. "Well, I wish you more luck than we've had, lad. There's only one ship in port right now, and though we've begged its captain to take us away from this evil land, he wouldn't even consider one of us."

"Not for anything," said Vigdis sadly.

"Not that we had much to offer," admitted Helga, "apart from our stories."

"Surely they'd be welcome on a long voyage," said Kjartan.

"You'd think they would be," agreed Helga. "But he's a cold man, this captain: he said he loves nothing better than silence."

"Then he'll like our nurse," said Kjartan chattily. "Would you believe it, ladies, she's so old that she's almost forgotten how to speak!"

"Is that so?" said Groa, with great interest. They jostled over to Ruadh where he sat wrapped up on his pony. Just then he broke into one of his fits of coughing, so that they all flinched away before they could see his face.

"I forgot to warn you," said Kjartan hastily. "She's already got a touch of sickness. I'd keep away from her if I were you, unless you want to catch her cough and risk your own health."

"And who's this?" asked Vigdis suddenly, as if they had only just noticed I was there. I trembled and hung my hooded face, fearing that, having once comforted me, she must surely recognise me again.

"Oh that's my sister," said Kjartan. "She's very shy, I'm afraid – she won't say a word to any stranger. In any case," he lowered his voice, yet kept it loud enough to ensure that I could hear, "she's not quite right in the head."

"What a shame!" Their toothless gums chewed us over

and over into a new story. I prayed that Ruadh at least should be miles away at sea before it reached my foster parents' ears.

"Let's be on our way, sisters," said Groa, shrinking again from his coughing. "We've a long road to tread."

She raised her arm to wave us off. As she did so, her ragged sleeve fell back to reveal a dazzle of gold – the bracelet I had given them earlier, in payment for their silence. Kjartan's eyes widened: before he could stop himself, he let out a cry of surprise.

"It's fit for a real lady, isn't it, lad?" said Groa proudly. "It was a gift to me from a local farm girl. Would you like to see it?"

Kjartan realised his mistake and shook his head, apologising for delaying them. But Groa, who probably had never possessed such a thing before, was eager to show it off.

"It's a real beauty," he assured them, as Groa turned it round before his eyes. We made to urge the horses onwards, but before we could, Helga said suspiciously, "Perhaps your sister would like to see it too, eh? Surely even a simpleton can enjoy such a treasure."

She thrust it under my face.

A hot blush crept up over my neck and into my cheeks, though still I hung my head. I tried to giggle foolishly, but this only increased Helga's mistrust.

"Look at it girl, won't you!" she cried angrily. She put a wizened hand under my chin, jerking my head up so that her yellowing eyes could see directly into mine. I stared back at her blankly, trying with all my might to convey that I bore no more than the vaguest resemblance to the Ingrid that they knew.

"See, sisters," said Helga with slow satisfaction, "see what she looks like!"

"Ah," said Vigdis, and I caught the tiniest edge of regret in her voice, "I wouldn't like to be in her shoes for anything."

"Having seen her now," said Groa knowingly, "we must feel sorry for what will become of them all."

Ruadh had another fit of coughing that at last sent the women scuttling off.

"*I* gave them that bracelet," I said, turning angrily to Kjartan. "It was all I had to pay for their silence, after they'd seen me returning home after you. And now, because of your thoughtlessness, you've ruined our plans and given us all away."

"They didn't recognise you, heiress," he replied sullenly. "You played your part too well."

"Then why are they rushing straight in the direction of my uncle's farm?"

"Hush," said Ruadh, "let's save our breath for the journey."

"Please let's hurry!" I insisted. "Those three could be at my farm in less than an hour. It wouldn't take long for my uncle and his men to saddle horses and follow us."

"Then we must ride like the wind!" declared Ruadh. "Come, my beauty," he whispered to his pony, "run swiftly to give an old king his last chance!"

So we broke into a gallop; and now Ruadh took the lead. An odd change had come about him. He sat

118

straighter in the saddle and did not need to stop so often.

But at last he slowed his horse and turned to us. His hollow cheeks were flushed and his eyes bright with effort.

"Can you smell it?" he exclaimed excitedly. "The sea! How it gladdens my heart and gives me courage. We must be almost there. Ingrid, will you lead the way?"

I took them down the steep cliff track, where the screaming birds circled round and round. At the bottom, still straining at its ropes in the shelter of the fjord, was Ulf Whitebeard's ship.

There was no sign of Ulf or his sons. But as we reached the bottom, his daughter Thurid suddenly appeared on the quayside.

"So you're back, Ingrid," she said coldly, coming up to meet us. She stopped by my horse and looked warily at the others. "Who have you brought?"

I was about to introduce Ruadh – but just in time remembered Thurid's part in the bargaining. She hovered there, a door to her father's presence, that would not open an inch unless I first presented the right key.

"This is my old nanny," I said, pointing to Ruadh, who had melted back into his disguise. "She's the one that your father's agreed to take on board his ship."

Thurid nodded. She seemed afraid to look at Ruadh. "And who's this? You only had permission to bring one person with you."

"Oh, this . . . this is . . ." Kjartan watched me, tight-lipped. The word 'slave' danced on the tip of my tongue. "This is my brother," I said quickly.

"What does he want?" demanded Thurid, still addressing only me.

"I want a place on your father's ship too," said Kjartan loudly. "In return, I'll work as hard as any man."

"I can't imagine what he'll say to that," said Thurid contemptuously. "You look so young and skinny."

Kjartan jumped in a rage from his horse, seized a boulder from the ground and flung it with all his might out into the fjord. It was a great heavy hunk of rock; yet it travelled smooth as a spear, far, far out, before it splashed into the water.

"That should have been *you*, for your rudeness," he said. "Now – go and fetch your father right now, and tell him that all three of us have arrived!"

She did not bat a single pale eyelash, but turned and went slowly into her father's workshop. Presently she returned with Ulf himself, and his five sons behind.

"So you've kept your word."

"This is my old nanny," I said, introducing Ruadh. "Will you take her?"

Ulf studied Ruadh long and hard.

"Throw back your hood, old woman. Let me see properly who would be taking up room on my ship."

Ruadh did so. He met Ulf's cold stare with his own, which was warm and tired as the end of summer.

"You look harmless," said Ulf wonderingly. "I've met enough scoundrels in my time to know one at once. You can join my crew, Irishman, if you'll keep hidden and silent until we've set you down and gone – and provided, of course, that Ingrid here has the payment we agreed."

120

From under my cloak I held out the golden chalice that I had guarded so carefully and so long. He took it from me and weighed it, first in one hand, then in the other, before sending one of his sons to fetch a set of scales. When he had tested it on these three times over, he said, "You've given me enough – and more. But Thurid tells me you've also brought another good-for-nothing that you want rid of?"

"My . . . brother here, sir," I ventured. "He was hoping you might take him on board too."

"I can *work* my way," said Kjartan eagerly. "I'm really strong – I've worked hard all my life!"

"Be that as it may," said Ulf doubtfully, turning to his sons. "Do we need another hand, boys?"

"Would you take into account that I've overpaid you?" I said.

Ulf shook his head. "What you've given me over isn't nearly enough for another."

"We don't want him," called one of his sons. "There's more than enough oarsmen already, and hardly an inch of room to spare."

"I could have brought you more gold," I pleaded. "If only I'd thought of it, I could have brought you double."

Ulf wavered. "You wore a pretty piece of gold-work around your neck once."

I hesitated, fingering my treasured Thor's Hammer. Kjartan's eyes darted to me, then quickly away. It did not weigh much, but it was as exquisitely made as any jewellery I had seen.

I unfastened it and handed it over.

121

"Thank you, Ingrid," whispered Kjartan.

Ulf took it and the sons crowded round to consider its worth.

As we waited there by the water, from far away there came a faint but distinct thundering of horse hooves. Ulf and his family showed no sign of recognition. But this was what the three of us had all been dreading: I saw Ruadh and Kjartan tense at the sound as I did.

"Father," said Thurid suddenly, "don't forget the third condition she's agreed to. How do we know even now that this so-called 'nanny' of hers isn't really the Sorcerer after all? She's got to offer herself publicly to his magic, as she swore to us that she would."

Ruadh looked astonished. But I stepped forward without hesitation and said, loud and clear to drown the sound of the fast approaching horses. "If the Sorcerer is here, let him work his spells on me!"

I saw Ulf, his sons and daughter start, and their faces stiffen with shock. Yet weren't these the very words they had commanded me to say? Perhaps they were startled at the riders' approach, for now they all stared straight past me and at the track behind.

Then a new voice broke the silence, my limbs turned to water, and my heart sped like a lost ship in the gales.

"That's good and generous of you, Ingrid; but I'd hate to harm someone as pretty and spirited as you."

I whirled round in a fizzing haze of terror.

Just behind us, mounted on an enormous, pitch-black horse, was the Sorcerer himself.

CHAPTER 14

The Last Meeting

Time stood still: we were frozen like statues. Even the wind dropped so that there was no sound except the laboured breath of Ruadh, and the steady clop-clop of other horses coming closer down the cliff path.

"Evil one," whispered Ruadh into the silence, "what do you want with us?"

"Oh, I'm just curious," replied the Sorcerer, looming over us on his horse, as crow-like as I remembered him. "I've heard rumours. They told me that someone else was being mistaken for me. I wanted to see what sort of a person it was." He laughed maliciously, so that his spittle fell onto Ruadh's pale, shorn cheeks. "You! – of all things, to find myself mistaken for a weak old man who dresses like a woman!"

Weary as he was, I was amazed to see how Ruadh controlled his temper at such mockery.

But Ruadh was looking straight past the Sorcerer. I tore my eyes away to follow his gaze. Clearly the three crones had lost no time in spreading news of our escape. For now here came Uncle Egil and Aunt Thorhalla, already riding to the bottom of the cliff, their faces wide-eyed with horror. Behind them came Grim Helgisson, wearing an inscrutable expression.

Grim got off his horse and strode towards our ill-mixed little group, running the three-fingered hand through his lank red hair.

"I have come . . ." he rasped, then broke off, staring from Ruadh to the Sorcerer and back again. "It was sworn to me," he began again, "that the outlaw I've been seeking for the past year was headed this way, hidden as a woman." He peered hard at Ruadh, taking in all his disguise and his foreign-looking features; and then he turned to the Sorcerer.

His eyes travelled slowly and fearlessly over the Sorcerer's flinty features, taking in the vacant eyes and the callous twist of his mouth.

"But *you*," he said, "it's you who have the mark of evil, not him."

"Come then," said the Sorcerer softly, "take me – if you can."

Grim flushed: he drew out his sword and began to approach.

He had scarcely taken two steps when the Sorcerer suddenly flung his cloak open – and drew from it a small glass bottle, holding it high in his gloved hand. It contained something green and foul-smelling that frothed threateningly over the top.

"Oh, you may be a good fighter," he hissed, "but you had better take care of my magic potion!"

We all jumped back, even Grim and Ulf's men, terrified to know what the stuff might be. The Sorcerer laughed drily at the fear he had put on all our faces. Then he dug in his spurs and made to gallop off.

But at that moment, Ruadh summoned up the last grains of his strength. He slipped quickly from his own pony, then staggered forward directly in front of the Sorcerer's great horse. There he stood, quivering with exhaustion: he drew his hand in the air in the shape of a cross, and shouted something in his own foreign tongue.

It looked as if the Sorcerer would ride straight onto him; but Ruadh's God must have heard his prayer. For the Sorcerer's horse stopped in the instant before its hooves would have trampled the Irishman down. It reared up, sweating with its own terror; and then Ulf Whitebeard's sons all came at it and hauled the Sorcerer from the saddle.

Thurid was screaming; Ruadh had collapsed; Aunt Thorhalla and Uncle Egil were yelling at me, "Come away, Ingrid, come away!" I heard them, but could not tear my eyes from what was happening.

Ulf's sons wrestled the Sorcerer until they had him imprisoned between them. But his strength – no doubt fed by dark powers – was phenomenal; and worse, he still clutched the phial of magic potion, so that they were all afraid to be near it.

"One touch of this," he hissed at them, "and your skin will turn to fire and burn away! One taste and you will be dead!" With a sudden jerk he made the little bottle spill over – and a few droplets of the liquid fell onto the skin of Ulf's eldest son.

Until then I had only half believed the Sorcerer's threat, but the effect of this left no doubt, for at once the son – great beefy fighter that he was – let go with a scream of agony. And where the liquid had touched him, I saw a dark hole form in his hand, surrounded by an oozing sore.

In that instant of terror, the brothers momentarily loosed their hold. The Sorcerer broke free of them and leapt back onto his horse.

"Who else wants a feel of it, eh?" he cried, brandishing the poison phial around. "Who would like to *taste* it? Who would like a taste of death?" He was riding towards Aunt Thorhalla now and leaned at her out of the saddle. "You, madam? Come, try it, taste it, my own poison recipe, brewed straight from mountain fire and molten mud!"

I've never seen my aunt look so terrified, never seen a group of fighting men so helpless. He dug in his spurs again and I believe every man would have let him gallop freely away, only suddenly a voice called, "I'll taste it, sir."

The Sorcerer jerked the reins in surprise, making his poor horse pull up short.

"What!" he sneered. "Is there really someone here as moon-crazed as myself? Who spoke?"

"Me," said Kjartan, coming forward. "*I'm* not afraid of you. I'm not afraid of anyone. Let me taste it."

The Sorcerer hesitated, incredulous.

"Go on," said Kjartan coming right up to him. "Give me a drink."

Then the next minute he had flung himself at the Sorcerer, and pulled him again from the saddle.

The Sorcerer was enraged. He drew his sword in his free hand and struck at Kjartan; he whipped the phial of potion round and round, trying to pour it on him – but Kjartan was too nimble. Though he had no weapon apart from his working knife, he darted wildly here and there, leading the Sorcerer in a macabre, deathly dance.

"Throw him a sword!" gasped Ruadh from the ground. But though each man held his own sword tightly before him, not one of them moved to Kjartan's aid. In furious disbelief, I turned on Grim. "In Thor's name, won't you help him?" I cried. I placed my own hand on his brawny fist and forced his grip from the sword-hilt. He was so surprised that he actually let me have it. I staggered a bit under the weight of it and began to inch towards Kjartan.

At last he was in reach. I thrust the hilt into his hands. But in those brief seconds both our attentions wavered. As Kjartan took the sword and stepped back, the Sorcerer's arm suddenly went round my own throat.

"One step closer to me, boy," he hissed at Kjartan, "and *she* shall be forced to drink my potion."

Everything became very still. I could hear the tension hissing in my ears. Kjartan stood frozen with doubt.

In the stillness I looked around. I could see every man ready to help me, yet each one afraid to make things worse by tipping the Sorcerer over the brink to kill me.

Now, hand on my shoulder, poison bottle held close to my face, the Sorcerer steered me back to his horse. I was in a dream, a nightmare. I let him lift me into the saddle, felt him swing himself up behind me, saw his lean hands come round on either side of me. One still taunted me with the magic potion, the other took up the reins.

It's the end of everything, I thought.

Then suddenly, just as we started off, I saw Kjartan's sword flash. It slashed at the hand that held the potion – once, twice. Quickly I turned my face away, petrified that some of it might spill into my mouth . . .

Something shattered. I looked down.

The little bottle had fallen and was broken into fragments. The poison had become no more than a foul green puddle, spreading slowly over the hard ground, and away.

The next moment, the startled horse reared up. I threw my arms around its neck and held on for dear life, but behind me the Sorcerer, one hand already bleeding from the sword blow, lost his balance and slid off.

He landed on his feet, pulled his own sword out with his good hand and lunged back at Kjartan. But the boy was too quick for him. Again he was dancing and darting about – this time, leading him steadily towards the edge of the cliff.

Grim strode after them, brandishing a borrowed sword. "Out of my way, slave boy," he shouted. "Stand back and let a real hero finish this job!"

Kjartan ignored him. Now he and the evil one were teetering on a precipice, their swords locked.

I dropped from the horse, for it was quietening now, and ran breathlessly towards them.

Even without his magic to hand, the Sorcerer was by far the stronger. But what Kjartan lacked in strength, he made up by tricks and dexterity. Of a sudden, he stepped aside. The Sorcerer, propelled by the force of his sword, fell forward into space as the fragile edge of the cliff crumbled away under his weight.

With a shriek that turned my blood to ice, he fell. Down, down, down he went to his death, into the deep dark reaches of the sea.

CHAPTER 15

Over the Sea

The deadly hush was broken by a heart-rending cry. I turned to see Ruadh huddled on the ground. Aunt Thorhalla and Thurid were standing uncertainly over him, as if they still feared that he was tainted with evil magic.

I ran across. His face was sickly white, but he saw me and his lips moved. I put my ear close, trying to catch his words, but it was no good. His breath was half broken. I lifted his shoulders onto my lap, trying to make him more comfortable; and all the while I was forcing back the tears, for he weighed no more than a month-old lamb.

"Bring him water!" I called to my aunt. But before she could stir, Kjartan was at my side, holding out a small flask from one of the horses' saddles. I took it and held it to Ruadh's lips.

At last the old man found his voice. "Dear Kjartan . . . surely . . . now they must give you . . . your freedom."

To my amazement, I saw tears shining in Kjartan's eyes.

"You'll be remembered," Ruadh whispered. "They'll make . . . poems about you."

Kjartan seemed to be struggling with something deep inside. He said bleakly, "Ruadh, are . . . are you going to die?"

"As the sun will set this evening," replied Ruadh, nodding calmly.

"You see . . . I want to give you something. It's not much. But . . . please take it. Perhaps," he said hoarsely, "perhaps you might ask them to . . . to put it with you in your . . . grave. For the next world."

From his neck he pulled the grimy leather thong that he always wore – the same that he had almost lost in his hurry to bring Ruadh the herbs.

"It's all I've got." He opened the rough little pouch that hung from its end, and I glimpsed a flash of gold. "Your hand," he murmured, and Ruadh held his hand out, trembling.

Into it Kjartan placed his secret treasure. It was a tiny golden cross.

Ruadh sat there, leaning in my arms, looking at the golden charm and rocking himself backwards and

131

forwards. Presently his eyes misted over until two huge tears rolled out, down over his thin, shaven cheeks.

Kjartan waited, embarrassed, looking at the ground.

"Is it . . . because you might not live to see Ireland again, friend?"

"No, I shan't ever sail there now, but what does it matter?" Now Ruadh began to laugh and weep at the same time. "You see, I have something better – far better than that!

He drew his hand away from Kjartan's, but still sat looking at the golden object it contained, as if this were the stuff of everlasting life.

"When I was a young man with a kingdom to my name," he said breathlessly, looking up at us all, "I had my new-born son baptised as a Christian, as is our way in Ireland. As a gift on that day, I gave him a golden cross, which is the symbol of our faith. When he was barely four years old, the Vikings came. They destroyed my kingdom and took my son away to sell him as a slave.

"But now – I declare with not a grain of doubt – here is that very same golden cross! So Kjartan – this brave and loyal young friend of mine, this noble wizard-killer – he surely must be my long-lost son, and the rightful heir to my kingdom!"

I heard Aunt Thorhalla's voice saying, "Well, well, well! what a wonder!" and a chorus of amazement broke out. Kjartan hid his face in his hands, his whole body shook; and then he fell onto his father's shoulder with a cry of gladness from his soul.

I was still supporting Ruadh, and with every minute

could feel the last strength draining out of him.

Gently he pushed Kjartan away.

"Go home and claim your kingdom, my son," he said, "and God help the man who stands in the path of Kjartan the Bold!"

Then he closed his eyes and died.

We all went away, into Ulf Whitebeard's house, leaving Kjartan alone for a while with his father and his grief.

At last he came to join us, standing pale and listless in the doorway. Uncle Egil went to him and slapped an arm about his shoulders.

"You're free!" he said grandly. "A slave no more – a free man from this very minute!" He looked across to Grim. "Um, you agree of course, Grim?"

"Oh, he can go," laughed Grim. "You don't owe me anything now, Egil. In fact, I think I'll keep well clear of your household from now on: there's too much excitement going on there for an old fellow like me!"

I breathed a sigh of relief.

Grim went on, "So, Kjartan Ruadhsson! You've inherited a throne across the sea, have you? Well, you know we don't think much of kings and queens here in Iceland – we believe that all free people should be equal. But I dare say there's something to be said for having a good bit of royal blood in your veins."

Kjartan nodded, still silent with misery. Then he suddenly cleared his throat and looked up at them. I was relieved to see some of the old insolence light one corner of his eye.

"Now I'm a free man," he said huskily, "and a . . . king! . . . will people do what I ask them?"

"Well now," said Aunt Thorhalla, "I'm sure they might do sometimes."

"Anyway, the lad ought to have a reward for his heroism," said Uncle Egil quickly. "What do you want?"

"Only this," said Kjartan. "That Ruadh – my father – should be buried as a Christian. I know he wants to go to his own Heaven – not to Valhalla with our – with your – gods."

"We'll do it," said Aunt Thorhalla at once. "I don't like these foreign ideas, I must say – but nevertheless, Kjartan, after all you've done, you must have the right to send your father on his last journey in the way you wish. Is there anything else?"

Kjartan looked at Ulf. "Can I take my father's place on your ship?"

Ulf gave his cold laugh. "What if I say no?"

"I'll fight you for it."

"Oh, you can have the place, your majesty – so long as you're not too proud to take your turn with the oars!"

So that was that.

We went home. Aunt Thorhalla sent riders out, and within two days they had found a man who called himself a Christian priest. We all went to Ruadh's funeral, which was a strange and moving event.

Afterwards, Kjartan packed his few belongings and prepared to ride back to Ulf's ship. He was dressed in a fine new set of clothes, presented by my aunt and uncle to start him on his way.

We all went out to see him off.

I watched him riding away along the coast road and suddenly was overcome by a great emptiness: there was still unfinished business between us. My aunt and uncle had already gone back to their work. I saddled Ice Star as fast as I could and went galloping after him.

He didn't turn as I caught him up, but just carried on, trotting steadily along.

"Well, well, well," I said when we were level, "so you were right, Kjartan – you *were* no slave after all." He didn't answer, so I went on, "What happened to all your grand talk of revenge against us, then?"

He shrugged. "I've got more urgent things to attend to, haven't I? There's a kingdom I have to find and make my own! Besides, I suppose your people were no worse to me than they had to be. And I don't think Ruadh – I mean, my father – would have wanted me to do them any harm. Fighting and revenge killings were against his religion, you know."

We rode on for a while in silence.

"I suppose I owe you a thank you, don't I, *Mistress*

Ingrid?"

"You don't need to call me that any more," I said.

"Oh, but I thought you liked it! You always spat at me if I forgot to give you your proper title."

I decided to ignore that.

"Yes," he went on, "you helped me quite a lot really. And my father. Especially at the end. I hope you didn't land yourself in too much trouble?"

"It's over now," I said, trying to sound as nonchalant as he always did. And then, to change the subject: "Have you heard? Since you destroyed the Sorcerer, the sickness is really going!"

"Well, that's hardly surprising."

"No . . . but, Kjartan, how could one man really have made so much evil? Where did he get so much power to cast his spells?"

Kjartan looked at me directly, with one eyebrow raised. "I reckon it's easy enough to sicken hundreds of sheep and pregnant women by slipping poison into a river or a well." He laughed scornfully. "Only idiots let themselves be scared of such a worm!"

"Well, I never ran away from him," I said.

He grunted and rode on.

"Are you coming much further with me?" he asked at length.

"I . . . I don't know. I really just came to say goodbye."

He reined in and turned to face me. He was flushed and his eyes shone brightly.

"So. Goodbye, Ingrid."

"I wish *I* were the one going," I said. "You're lucky,

sailing to adventure in a new land. They won't let *me* go anywhere or do anything until I come of age." Our eyes met. "I wonder if you'll have won your kingdom back by then?"

"If you really want to know, you'll have to come over the sea and find out for yourself, won't you, Ingrid?" He grinned; then the next moment he dug in his heels so hard that his horse went streaking off as if there were a storm inside it.

I stood and watched him disappear.

"One day the humblest of men shall be your lord," the Sorcerer had told me; and though his evil was gone for ever, thanks to Kjartan the Bold, I was still haunted by his prophecy.

I turned and rode slowly back towards my own farm; and as the distance between us grew, an idea began to form in my mind.

Well! I thought, when I'm a woman, why shouldn't I go travelling myself, southwards over the sea to Ireland? That's the only way to find out for sure what happens to this so-called king, who once slew a monster when all the Icelanders had failed. My heart was singing. And who knows – perhaps I might even persuade him to give me a high-seat next to his own, right at the head of his kingdom!

About this Story

Sorcery and Gold is set in Iceland during the Viking Age – about a thousand years ago.

Iceland is a wild and savagely beautiful island, which lies just below the Arctic Circle. Some of it is lush pasture, ideal for sheep farming. But beyond this are many extraordinary and inhospitable landscapes: permanently frozen ice-caps and glaciers, active volcanoes, bleak deserts of solidified lava, bare mountains, pools of boiling mud and steaming hot springs.

Through most of history, Iceland was uninhabited. But during the late ninth century AD it began to be settled by farming families from Norway, and it soon became one of the most important centres of the Viking world. From here explorers sailed further westward to Greenland, and then on to become the first Europeans to reach North America.

The people who settled in Iceland had to travel across the heaving North Atlantic ocean in simple open ships. They were physically tough and independently minded. They settled all over the country and made their livings from sheep farming, and from spinning and weaving the sheep's fleece into woollen cloth. But some families also grew very rich with gold and silver treasure, stolen by their men in the infamous Viking raids which, for about three hundred years, terrorised people in many other parts of Europe. Rich families such as Ingrid's had both paid servants and slaves (many brought from Ireland) to help with the house and farm work.

The first Icelanders followed the old Norse religion, worshipping many gods and goddesses. These included Thor, the popular god of Thunder, whose symbol was a hammer, and Odin, the mysterious All-Father. Most people were highly superstitious and readily believed in the supernatural. However, around the time when this story is set, Christianity was just beginning to arrive in Iceland from the rest of Europe.

The Icelanders respected powerful local men called chieftains, but they had no king or queen. Instead they ordered their own affairs through the *Althing* or Great Assembly, which was attended by men and women from all over the country every summer. It was also the main social event of the year, when people from remotely scattered farms could get together to exchange gossip, arrange marriages and settle feuds. Although violence was common, most people tried to follow a strict code of honour. Women enjoyed a degree of independence and respect which was unusual elsewhere until modern times.